JAMESTOWN EDUCATION

W9-BEU-615

# Teacher's Guide

# English, Yes!

## Learning English Through Literature

**Level 3: Beginning**

**Mc Graw Hill** **Glencoe**

New York, New York   Columbus, Ohio   Chicago, Illinois   Peoria, Illinois   Woodland Hills, California

JAMESTOWN 🚢 EDUCATION

Cover photo illustration: Third Eye Image/Solus Photography/Veer

The McGraw-Hill Companies

Send all inquiries to:
Glencoe/McGraw-Hill
8787 Orion Place
Columbus, OH 43240-4027

ISBN 0-07-860028-6
Printed in the United States of America.

2  3  4  5  6  7  8  9  10  021  08  07  06

# Contents

# About the *English, Yes!* Program

*English, Yes!* is a literature-based program for readers who need help improving their basic English skills. Each book in the series contains outstanding readability-controlled stories based on the works of famous writers. Passages in the Introductory level are kept very short; they average 400 words. Those in the Beginning and Intermediate levels have been divided into a number of short, illustrated sections to make them more manageable for limited English proficient (LEP) students. The Advanced and Transitional levels contain poetry in addition to stories.

The Introductory, Beginning, and Intermediate levels use line reference numbers in the margins of the stories. These are useful not only in helping the reader locate specific answers but also in providing easy reference for reinforcement and review. These books also contain certain words and phrases printed in **boldface** type. This identifies vocabulary and idioms that are tested in the multiple-choice comprehension check following each section.

In addition to these books, a Basic level is available for those students who are just beginning to learn English. It begins with units on naming the letters of the alphabet, working with numbers, and filling out forms. Additional units focus on basic vocabulary and grammar. The book emphasizes the skills that new immigrants need to adapt to U.S. secondary schools and other aspects of U.S. society and culture.

Each section in every book except Basic is followed by a comprehensive three-part skills check using the acronym *YES*. It has been especially developed to meet the needs of LEP readers and is consistent with the general scope and sequence of ESL curricula.

## You Can Answer These Questions
Ten multiple-choice questions review reading comprehension, vocabulary, and idioms in the section just completed. A Score Chart at the end of each Student Book permits readers to enter their scores and record their progress.

## Exercises to Help You
Varied exercises use directed writing activities for mastery of story comprehension, sentence structure, verb tenses, parts of speech, and punctuation.

## Sharing with Others
Cooperative learning and shared learning activities developed from the content provide opportunities for participants to work together to improve their listening, speaking, and writing skills.

The vocabulary has been drawn primarily from core word lists for beginning, intermediate, and advanced level students.

# About the *English, Yes!* Teacher's Guide

In addition to full instructions for presenting the stories and skills, this Teacher's Guide contains a Placement Test which will assist you in determining which level of *English, Yes!* is best suited for an individual student. Full instructions are found on page vi.

The introduction to each story contains these features.

The **Planning Guide** lists the skills and strategies taught in that story or unit.

The **Vocabulary** lists the words and idioms that are checked in the exercises. They are arranged in groups by subject matter.

A **Story Synopsis** provides a brief retelling of the main events of the story.

**About the Author** presents background information about each author along with suggested ways to share this information with students.

**Introducing the Story** contains activities that activate prior knowledge and build background. A variety of **Options** provide additional brainstorming and/or writing activities to further lead students into the selection.

The teaching material for each section contains these features.

A **Warm Up** provides a number of activities to develop vocabulary, activate prior knowledge, and introduce the selection. These activities typically include the use of graphic organizers, critical thinking, and language across the curriculum.

**Read the Selection** contains suggestions for leading the students through the material in small, easy to digest sections. Comprehension questions are provided for each section along with information on modeling strategies, using graphic organizers, and promoting critical thinking.

**You Can Answer These Questions** contains the answers to the comprehension check at the end of each section.

**Exercises to Help You** provides suggestions for teaching the grammar highlighted in the exercises and gives the answers to those exercises.

**Sharing with Others** gives tips on presenting and expanding that section of the lesson in the Student Book.

**Assessment** pages appear in the Teacher's Guide at the ends of the units. Each assessment page checks vocabulary, grammar, and comprehension. This page may be photocopied.

# About the *English, Yes!* Placement Tests

*English, Yes!* provides two Placement Tests. The first test appears in the Introductory, Beginning, and Intermediate A Teacher's Guides. The second test appears in the Intermediate B, Advanced, and Transitional Teacher's Guides.

Each test contains reading passages at three progressive levels of difficulty, followed by five multiple choice questions and three open-ended questions about the passage. Answers to the multiple choice questions will help you judge reading comprehension. Responses to the open-ended questions will help you judge production ability.

## Guidelines for Testing

Try to make the testing conditions as relaxed as possible. Students almost always view a test as a threatening situation. You will want to do everything you can to relieve tension. Smile. Try to maintain a conversational tone.

First, ask basic questions. Find out the student's name, address, and favorite subject in school. Give the student a short form in which to fill out some basic personal information. If the student is unable to answer your questions or complete the form, start him or her in the Level 1: Basic.

If the student can complete these tasks, give him or her the first Placement Test. Allow about twenty minutes for the student to complete the test. If at any point the student seems frustrated, stop the test.

## Scoring

There is a total of 3 pages with 24 questions: 5 multiple choice and 3 open ended on each page. Score the test and review grammar, usage, and mechanics. Use this scale to place the student in the appropriate level of *English, Yes!*

> 0–5 correct answers—Level 2: Introductory
> Student uses very limited vocabulary and produces only sentence fragments. He or she demonstrates little control over tenses or other grammatical features.

> 6–10 correct answers—Level 3: Beginning
> Student uses basic, limited vocabulary; writes run-ons and fragments using non-standard word order. Also makes many errors in inflections, agreement, and word meaning.

> 11–15 correct answers—Level 4: Intermediate A
> Student uses adequate, functional vocabulary and mostly standard word order. May make some errors in inflections, agreement, and word meaning.

If a student has 16 or more correct answers, give him or her the second Placement Test.

## Placement Test Answer Key

### Page vii

1. b     2. a     3. c     4. a     5. a

Students' answers will vary. Suggested answers:

6. The judge made good decisions.
7. The traveler sat near a food stand. He ate rice and vegetables. He smelled the fish.
8. The person told the traveler and owner to go to the judge.

### Page viii

1. c     2. b     3. c     4. a     5. a

Students' answers will vary. Suggested answers:

6. Pakhom dreamed of having much land.
7. The man thought the Bashkirs were stupid because they sold land for very little money.
8. Pakhom should make friends with the Chief of the Bashkirs so that he can get land.

### Page ix

1. a     2. b     3. c     4. c     5. a

Students' answers will vary. Suggested answers:

6. Many years ago, the men nearly killed each other fighting over her.
7. No, he didn't. The room was dark, and filled with spider webs and dust.
8. No, he isn't married. He still has a painting on the wall of the woman he was going to marry fifty years ago.

# Placement Test

*Read these directions silently while your teacher reads them aloud:*

*Read the paragraphs. They are from a story in the Level 2 book. Then read all of the questions. Choose the correct answer to each question; then circle the letter of the correct answer. When you have finished, turn the page and continue the test.*

Long ago, in Asia, there was a famous judge. People respected her. She made good decisions. She knew the law, and she helped the poor.

One day, a poor traveler was in the market of the town. He sat near a food stand. The owner of the stand was cooking fish.

The traveler ate his own rice and vegetables. The fish smelled good. The traveler ate his food, and he enjoyed the smell of the fish. He ate slowly. He thought of the tasty fish.

Suddenly the owner of the stand came up to the traveler. "You have to pay me for the smell of my fish." The traveler replied, "But I didn't eat anything. So I don't have to pay you."

The pair started to argue in the market. Soon a crowd gathered. A person in the crowd said, "This is a difficult problem. Go to our judge."

1.  The judge helped
    a.  the rich.
    b.  the poor.
    c.  the owner.

2.  The traveler ate
    a.  his own food.
    b.  fish.
    c.  nothing.

3.  The judge was
    a.  an owner.
    b.  a man.
    c.  a woman.

4.  The traveler sat near a food stand. As it is used here, the word *stand* means
    a.  a place where people buy things.
    b.  a place where people cannot sit.
    c.  a place where a judge works.

5.  The owner wanted the traveler to
    a.  pay for a smell.
    b.  buy fish.
    c.  talk to the judge.

*Now answer these questions about the story on the lines below. Write as much as you can.*

6.  What did the judge make? _____

_____

7.  What did the traveler do at the market? _____

_____

8.  What did a person tell the traveler and the owner to do? _____

_____

*Read the paragraphs. They are from a story in the Level 3 book. Then read all of the questions. Choose the correct answer to each question; then circle the letter of the correct answer. When you have finished, turn the page and continue the test.*

Pakhom was a poor farmer, but he dreamed of having much land. Pakhom's farm was very small. It was less than an acre. One day a traveler stopped at Pakhom's farm. The traveler needed food for his horse. Pakhom gave the horse some oats. Then Pakhom and the man drank tea and talked.

The man said, "I am returning from a land that is far away. It is in the south of Russia. It is called the Land of the Bashkirs." The man told Pakhom that he had bought a piece of land from the Bashkirs. It was a very large piece of land—more than 1,500 acres. The land was cheap. It was very cheap. It cost only 500 rubles. Pakhom was interested in what the traveler said.

The man said, "The Bashkirs are very stupid. They will sell you land for very little money. All you need to do is make friends with their Chief. I gave them some tea and some presents. Then they sold me a large piece of land for almost nothing."

1. Pakhom's small farm was less than an acre. The word *acre* means
   a. the number of cows on a farm.
   b. the number of people in a village.
   c. the size of a piece of land.

2. The traveler stopped at Pakhom's farm to
   a. rest there for the night.
   b. get food for his horse.
   c. buy another horse.

3. The Land of the Bashkirs is
   a. near Pakhom's farm.
   b. in northern Russia.
   c. far away.

4. The land was cheap. The word *cheap* means
   a. costs a little money.
   b. costs a lot of money.
   c. looks pretty.

5. The man gave the Bashkirs
   a. tea and presents.
   b. money and clothes.
   c. food and horses.

*Now answer these questions about the story on the lines below. Write as much as you can.*

6. What did Pakhom dream of having? _____

_____

7. Why did the man think that the Bashkirs were stupid? _____

_____

8. Why should Pakhom make friends with the Chief of the Bashkirs? _____

_____

*Read the paragraphs. They are from a story in the Level Four book. Then read all of the questions. Choose the correct answer to each question, then circle the letter of the correct answer. When you have finished, the test is complete.*

Dr. Heidegger was a strange old man. Once, he invited four friends to meet with him at his house. All of these people had lived very sad and unfortunate lives.

Years ago, Mr. Medbourne had been a rich man. But because he was greedy, he made some bad business deals and lost his fortune. Now he had to beg for money. Mr. Gascon had been a famous politician. But he was dishonest. He was caught stealing money and went to jail. Now he was poor and lived in shame. Colonel Killigrew was once a great soldier. But he spent his life eating and drinking too much. Now his health was bad, and he was sick all the time.

As for the Widow Wycherly, she was once quite beautiful. But she was very conceited. She thought she was the most beautiful woman in town. She was not beautiful now. The three men had each loved her very much when they were young. Once, they almost killed each other fighting over her. But that was many years ago.

Dr. Heidegger's laboratory was an unusual place. It was a large, dark room filled with spider webs and dust. Around the walls stood tall wooden bookcases that were filled with books. Between two of the bookcases, there was a large painting of a young woman in a long silk dress. More than fifty years ago, Dr. Heidegger was going to marry this woman. The day before their wedding, she suddenly became ill. Dr. Heidegger gave her some medicine, but she died that evening.

1. All of these people had lived very sad and unfortunate lives. The word *unfortunate* means
   a. not lucky.
   b. not happy.
   c. very short.

2. Mr. Medbourne lost his fortune because
   a. he was mean.
   b. he was greedy.
   c. he was not lucky.

3. Colonel Killigrew is sick all the time because
   a. he was a soldier.
   b. he was poor.
   c. he spent his life eating and drinking too much.

4. The Widow Wycherly was once
   a. very rich.
   b. very fat.
   c. very beautiful.

5. Dr. Heidegger's laboratory was
   a. very dirty.
   b. very clean.
   c. very sunny.

*Now answer these questions about the story on the lines below. Write as much as you can.*

6. What happened many years ago that would make Widow Wycherly think she was the most beautiful woman in town? _____

_____

7. Did Dr. Heidegger usually invite people to his laboratory? What clues in the story helped you decide?

_____

_____

8. Do you think Dr. Heidegger is married now? Why or why not? _____

_____

**Venn Diagram**

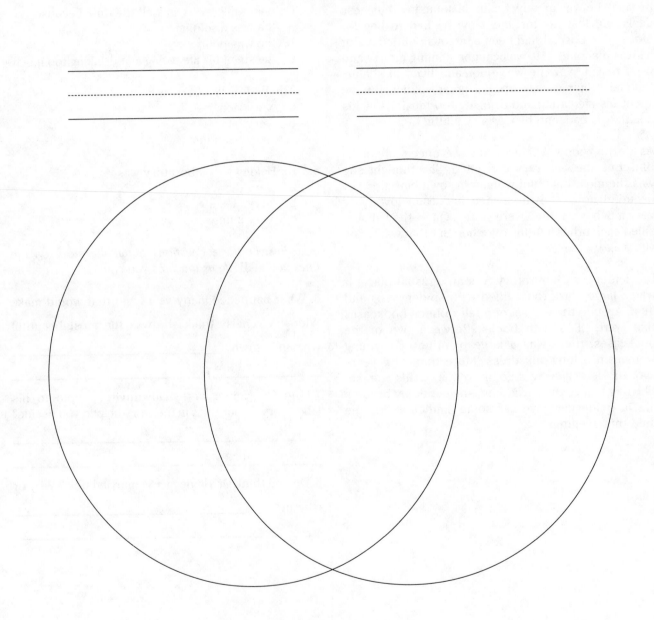

**T-Chart**

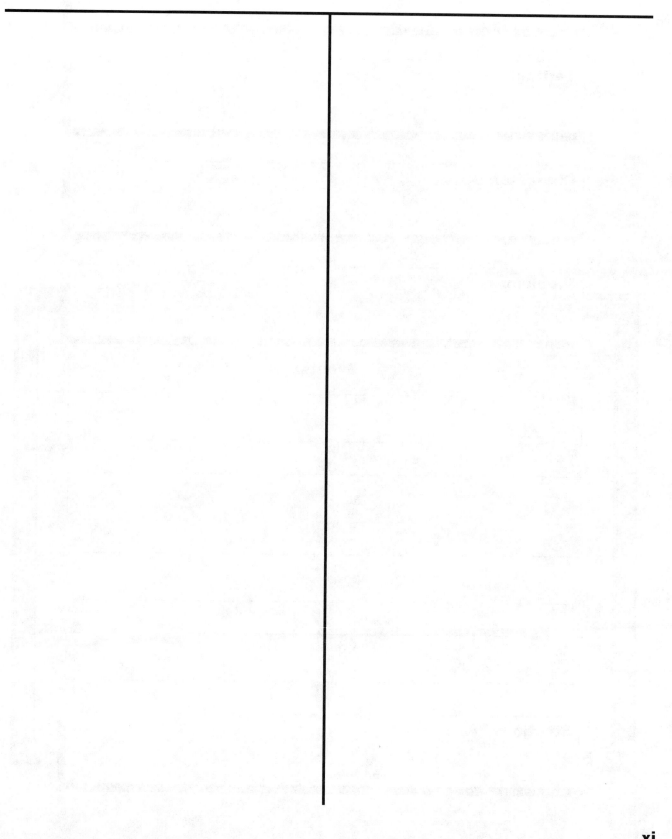

# Story Elements Chart

**Title:**

**Setting:**

**Characters:**

**Problem:**

## Events:

**Solution:**

**Main Idea Chart**

**Main Idea**

**Details**

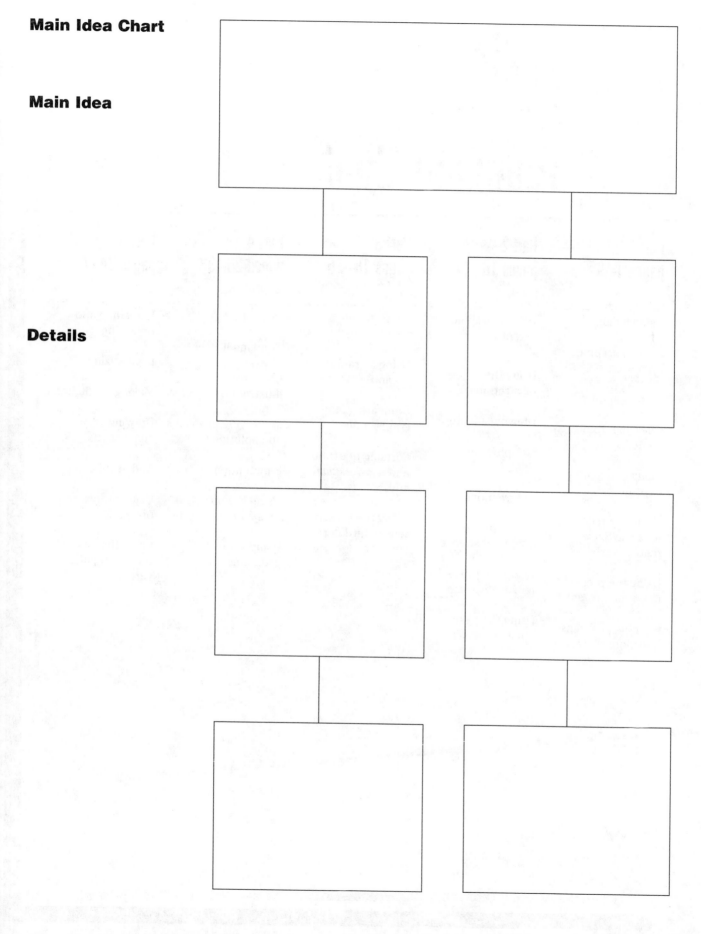

# Wolf

# Planning Guide

| Part 1 pages 1–9 | Part 2 pages 10–17 | Part 3 pages 18–25 | Part 4 pages 26–33 | Part 5 pages 34–41 |
|---|---|---|---|---|
| Using a map | Using a graphic organizer | Summarizing and sequencing | Dramatizing | Rereading and reviewing |
| Using a graphic organizer | Using the illustrations | Using a graphic organizer | Thinking it over | Dramatizing |
| Word mapping | Drawing a picture | Comparing and contrasting | Using the illustrations | Making predictions |
| Guessing from context | Stopping and thinking | Forming questions and answers: *why* and *because* | Identifying problems and solutions | Drawing conclusions |
| Using conventions of print | Contractions | Using the present tense: third person singular | Punctuation | Apostrophes |
| Using the past tense: *was/were*, regular verbs | Using the past continuous tense | | Using the past tense: regular verbs | Using prepositions of location |
| Using the present tense: *am, is, are* | Using the present tense: *have/has* | | Using subject pronouns | Using the past tense: irregular verbs |
| Forming past tense questions: *was/were* | Using the past tense: *was/were* | | | |

# Vocabulary

## Story Words

to choose
to continue
to drag
to earn
to feed
to grab
to growl
to obey
to prove

curve
dinner
dog
door
food
ground
hammer
handkerchief
leader
log
minute
neighbor
night
path
sled
team

married
plenty
stolen
straight
worth

nearby
suddenly

## Words Relating to Feelings

to care
to suffer
to understand

lazy
shocked
sick
starved

## Words Relating to Body Parts

to lick
to nod

fist
mouth
paw
shoulder
teeth
tongue

## Idioms

to catch up
to drop in
to make up his mind
to shake hands
to take long walks

all right
at once
right away

# Wolf

pages 1–41

## Story Synopsis

One night Madge and Walt, a married couple who live in California, find a lost, unfriendly dog in their yard. The dog looks hungry, so Madge and Walt give it some food. They name the dog Wolf because it eats like a wolf and looks like a wolf. Wolf becomes friendly and goes for walks in the woods with Madge and Walt. One day they meet a man from Alaska, Skiff Miller. Skiff recognizes Wolf as a dog of his called Brown. Brown had been stolen from Skiff three years before. Skiff wants to take Wolf back to Alaska with him, but Madge and Walt want to keep the dog. After a heated argument, Walt and Skiff decide to let the dog choose where it wants to live. Wolf is torn between the two sides but finally runs down the road after Skiff.

## About the Author

Jack London was born in San Francisco, California, in 1876. He went to the Klondike and Alaska in the 1897 Gold Rush. He later traveled to the South Pacific and Japan. He wrote many exciting adventure novels about people struggling against nature, among them *The Call of the Wild, White Fang,* and *The Sea-Wolf.* Jack London died in 1916.

Bring in a world map and invite students to locate some of the places Jack London lived and visited. Help students discuss the modes of transportation that would have been used at those times.

If possible, find a picture of Jack London. Have students describe the picture and then discuss personality traits and skills he must have had to travel and live as he did.

Have students make a time line for Jack London's life. You may want to have students use resource materials to look up information and dates about his life. Ask students to summarize Jack London's life based on the information on their time line.

# Introducing the Story

Have students look at the opening illustration on page vi. Guide discussion of the characters and setting pictured. Encourage students to point out and comment on details in the picture. Use the questions on page 1 to help focus the discussion.

*Note:* Point out to students that there are no "right" answers to these questions; they are making predictions, and they will find out if their predictions are correct when they read the story. Help students support their answers with details from the picture, and accept all logical answers.

## Vocabulary Option

Encourage students to brainstorm words that they associate with *dog.* Make a list of students' ideas on the board. If needed, use questions to guide the activity: What does a dog look like? What can dogs do? Why do people have dogs? You may want to suggest some of the key vocabulary words from the story to add to the list.

## Writing Option

Invite students to write a description of one of the characters (or the dog) from the illustration. Students may work alone or in pairs to describe the character's physical appearance and guess who the character is, what his or her occupation is, and where he or she lives. Suggest that students list their ideas before writing.

# Wolf

**Part One, pages 1-9**

## Warm Up

Use any or all of the activities below.

### Using a Map

Have students find California and Alaska on a map. Encourage students to use the map information and their own prior knowledge to compare the two locations in terms of climate, environment, and living conditions.

### Using a Graphic Organizer

Students can record information about California and Alaska on a Venn diagram, page x. Invite students to make comparative statements about the two states based on the diagram.

### Word Mapping

As a group, begin a word map for *dog*, using some of the words and phrases that students suggested in the Vocabulary Option. Guide students to group words together into categories for the mapping.

### Language Across the Curriculum
### Science: Animal Body Parts

Help students make a list of body parts for various animals, including dogs. Then help them determine which words are the same for animals and humans, and which are different. For example, *paw* is used instead of *hand* for dogs and cats.

## Read the Selection

Have students follow along on page 2 of their books as you read lines 1–17 aloud or play track 1 on the Level Three CD. Check students' understanding of the passage by asking any or all of the following questions.

1. What were the names of the man and woman?
2. Where did Madge and Walt live?
3. Why did they wake up one night?
4. What did they see outside?
5. Was the dog friendly or angry?

Check understanding of key vocabulary. Reassure students that it is not necessary to know the meaning of every word to get the general meaning of a passage.

Continue by reading lines 18–43 on pages 2–3 or by playing track 2 on the Level Three CD. Check for understanding using any or all of the following questions.

1. What did Madge and Walt give the dog to eat?
2. Why did Madge name the dog "Wolf"?
3. Who was Mrs. Johnson?
4. Where did she think Wolf was from?

After reading the passage, guide students to summarize the story so far. As students retell the important events and information, write the key ideas on the board and review key vocabulary.

## Model a Strategy:
## Guessing from Context

Write the word *sled* on the board and ask students to find it in line 41 on page 3. Say: "A sled is something that big dogs can pull. Mrs. Johnson saw dogs like Wolf pulling sleds in Alaska. I know that dogs can pull wagons. Wagons have wheels. But there's a lot of snow in Alaska, and wheels don't go well in the snow. Maybe a sled is like a wagon but it has something to slide on instead of wheels."

Guide students to notice how information in the story can sometimes be used to help understand new words. If possible, bring in a picture of a sled and dog team to clarify the meaning of the word.

## Using Conventions of Print

Draw students' attention to the use of dark **(boldface)** type to highlight important new vocabulary. Explain that they will be using these words in the exercises.

## Y ou Can Answer These Questions

Students can do the activity in class or as homework.

| | | | |
|---|---|---|---|
| 1. | a | 6. | c |
| 2. | a | 7. | a |
| 3. | c | 8. | b |
| 4. | b | 9. | c |
| 5. | a | 10. | b |

## E xercises to Help You

### Using the Past Tense:
### *was/were*, Regular Verbs

Model the use of *was/were* to talk about a past time.

> Yesterday the dog *was* hungry.

> Walt and Madge *were* sorry for the dog.

Explain the form of regular past tense verbs in affirmative statements.

> Walt and Madge *watched* the dog.

> They *wanted* to help the dog.

> The dog *growled* at them.

Guide students to notice the *-ed* ending as you say the past tense statements.

Encourage students to look back through pages 2–3 for other examples of *was/were* and the past tense of regular verbs.

Ask students to do Exercises A, B, and C on pages 5–7. Students may work in pairs or groups to complete them or work individually on the exercises for homework.

*Exercise A*

Students' sentences will vary. Suggested answers:

1. The man's name was Walt.
2. The woman's name was Madge.
3. The dog's name was Wolf.
4. They lived in California.
5. A loud sound woke them up.
6. They saw a large, brown dog.
7. They gave the dog some bread and milk.
8. The dog ate all the food.
9. Mrs. Johnson's brother lived in Alaska.
10. Mrs. Johnson visited her brother last year.

*Exercise B*

1. b  Madge and Walt were married.
2. a  They lived in California.
3. d  A loud sound woke them up.
4. c  They walked toward the dog.
5. c  The dog was not friendly.
6. a  They gave it some bread and milk.
7. d  Madge and Walt looked out the window.
8. b  The next morning they fed Wolf again.

*Exercise C*

| | | | |
|---|---|---|---|
| 1. | married | 5. | ground |
| 2. | night | 6. | food |
| 3. | door | 7. | neighbor |
| 4. | dog | 8. | sleds |

**Using the Present Tense: *am, is, are***

Help students talk about themselves and the characters in the story using the present tense of the verb *to be*. Write examples on the board and guide students to notice the forms of the verb and the corresponding subject pronouns.

> Madge and Walt *are* married.
>
> Mrs. Johnson *is* a neighbor.
>
> I *am* not from Alaska.
>
> *Are* you hungry?

Write verb forms, character names, and predicates on the board. Have students create sentences by choosing one item from each of the categories.

**Forming Past Tense Questions: *was/were***

Write some examples of past tense statements and questions with *was/were* on the board.

> The dog *was* lost.
> *Was* the dog lost?
>
> Madge and Walt *were* surprised.
> *Were* Madge and Walt surprised?

Guide students to notice the change in word order from the affirmative statement to the question form. Invite students to give other examples using the characters and information from the story.

Assign Exercises D, E, and F on pages 7–9.

*Exercise D*

| | | | |
|---|---|---|---|
| 1. | is | 5. | is |
| 2. | are | 6. | am |
| 3. | is | 7. | is |
| 4. | are | | |

*Exercise E*

1. Was the dog tired?
2. Was the dog hungry?
3. Was the dog lost?
4. Was the dog outside the house?
5. Were Madge and Walt married?
6. Was the dog a little more friendly?
7. Were Madge and Walt sleeping?
8. Was Mrs. Johnson surprised?
9. Was Mrs. Johnson's brother in Alaska?
10. Were Madge and Walt surprised, too?

*Exercise F*
Students' sentences will vary.

# **S**haring with Others

Arrange students in pairs or in small groups to discuss the answers to the questions in the activity on page 9. Students can use vocabulary from the *dog* word map that they started in the Warm Up.

After students decide on their topic, give them a graphic organizer such as the Main Idea chart, page 1 in the Teacher's Guide (p. T1), to record their ideas before actually writing.

Invite students to share their writing by reading it aloud. As an alternative, make an exhibit of the writing on a bulletin board or on a table for students to look through. ■

# Wolf

Part Two, pages 10–17

## Warm Up

Use any or all of the activities below.

### Using a Graphic Organizer

Ask students to retell the first part of the story. Help students identify the main characters, setting, and events. Demonstrate how to create a story map using the Story Elements chart on page xii. Help students fill in the information, and encourage them to add events as they read the rest of the story.

### Using the Illustrations

Have students look at the illustration on page 11. Guide discussion of the scene and help students describe the physical appearance of the character. Help them create questions they would like answered about the character, and write the questions on the board for later reference.

### Drawing a Picture

Give students paper and ask them to draw a picture of a forest or woods. Encourage students to include things they might see and things people might do in the woods. Invite students to share and explain their drawings. You may want to bring in a picture of a woodland scene and discuss similarities and differences between the picture and students' drawings.

## Language Across the Curriculum
## Science: Seasons and Weather

Invite students to talk about their favorite seasons. Make a chart with the names of the seasons as headings and help students list seasonal weather conditions.

## Read the Selection

Play track 3 on the CD or read aloud lines 1–25 as students follow along on page 10 of their books. Use questions such as the ones below to check students' understanding of the passage.

1. Was Wolf friendly to Madge and Walt?
2. What did Wolf do when Madge and Walt called him?
3. Whom did Walt and Madge meet in the woods? What did he look like?

Check that students understand key vocabulary in the selection. Remind students to read for the general meaning and to not be concerned about understanding every word in the passage. Encourage students to suggest what will happen when Wolf sees the man.

Play CD track 4 or read lines 26–48 on pages 10–11. Check students' comprehension of the passage by using any or all of the following questions.

1. Whom was the man looking for?
2. What was his name? Where was he from?
3. What did Skiff Miller stare at?

Guide students in summarizing the information and events of the selection. Write the main ideas on the board and review key vocabulary. Check to see if any of the questions students asked about the illustrations were answered in this selection.

### Model a Strategy: Stopping and Thinking

Say: "When I read a story, sometimes I need to think about what has happened and what might happen next. In this story, I learned that Wolf is probably from Alaska. This new character, Skiff Miller, is also from Alaska. Skiff Miller stares at Wolf. I wonder why he is looking at Wolf so long. Maybe Miller knows Wolf. Wolf was not friendly to Madge and Walt, and he still does not come close to them. I wonder how Wolf will behave towards Skiff Miller. Will Wolf stay far away from him?"

Encourage students to think about possible reactions from the dog toward Skiff Miller based on what they know from the story.

### Contractions

Guide students to notice contractions in the selection. Write examples on the board: *I'm*, *don't*, *it's*. Explain the use of the apostrophe to indicate letters that are omitted. Discuss how contractions are often used in speech. Ask students to find other examples in the passage and help them decide what the original words are.

## You Can Answer These Questions

Students can do the activity in class or as homework.

| | |
|---|---|
| 1. a | 6. a |
| 2. b | 7. a |
| 3. b | 8. c |
| 4. b | 9. b |
| 5. c | 10. c |

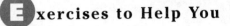

## Exercises to Help You

### Using the Past Continuous Tense

Model the use of the past continuous tense to talk about an action that was in progress or continuing in the past.

The dog *was eating* some bread.

They *were looking* for the dog.

Point out the use of *was/were* and the *-ing* form of the verb. Have students look back through pages 10–11 for other examples of the past continuous tense.

Students can do Exercises A, B, and C on pages 13–15. You may want to arrange students in pairs or groups to complete the exercises as classwork or assign them for homework.

*Exercise A*

Students' sentences will vary. Suggested answers:

1. Madge and Walt fed Wolf every day.
2. Walt had a hammer in his hand.
3. Walt was fixing the fence.
4. Miller was holding his hat in his hand.
5. Miller took a red handkerchief out of his pocket.
6. Miller wiped his face with the handkerchief.
7. Miller was looking for his sister.
8. Miller had important business in Alaska.

*Exercise B*

1. c   Madge and Walt took long walks with Wolf.
2. a   Wolf was sitting on top of a large rock.
3. d   The man came out of the woods.
4. b   They thought that Skiff Miller was very strong.
5. b   Madge and Walt did not know the man.

6. d Skiff Miller was holding his hat in his hand.
7. c Walt pointed to a path near a tree.
8. a Miller kept staring at the dog.

### Exercise C

1. mouth
2. shoulders
3. nearby
4. hammer
5. continued
6. dinner

## Using the Present Tense: *have/has*

Ask questions about students and the story characters to elicit sentences using the present tense of the verb *to have*. Say: "Do you have a hat or a handkerchief?" "Does Skiff Miller have a brother or a sister?" Write responses on the board. Point out the two forms of the verb (*have/has*) and invite students to create additional sentences about themselves and the story characters using the verb forms.

I *have* a hat.

You *have* a brother.

Skiff Miller *has* a sister.

We *have* short hair.

Walt and Madge *have* a dog.

## Using the Past Tense: *was/were*

Ask students questions in the past tense to help them give examples of *was/were*. Ask: "What was Walt fixing with the hammer?" "Where were Madge and Walt walking?"

Walt *was* fixing a fence.

Madge and Walt *were* walking down a road.

After you write the responses, help students to notice the use of *was* with singular subjects and *were* with plural subjects and with *you*. Explain that *was/were* are used to describe things in the past.

Assign Exercises D, E, and F on pages 15–17.

### Exercise D
### Part A

1. has
2. has
3. has
4. have
5. have

### Exercise D
### Part B

1. was
2. was
3. were
4. was
5. was
6. was
7. were

### Exercise E

1. warm
2. tall
3. important
4. black
5. large

### Exercise F

Students' sentences will vary.

## haring with Others

Have students reread Skiff's response about the weather in lines 27–28 on page 10. Guide discussion of why he prefers cold weather. Then have students work in pairs or small groups as they discuss the questions on page 17.

Have students choose one of the topics to write about. Students can use the Main Idea chart, page T1, to record their ideas before writing. Encourage students to give reasons for their own preferences when they write.

Invite students to illustrate their writing. Make a display of the illustrations and writings or have students share their work in small groups. ■

# Wolf

## Warm Up

Use any or all of the activities below.

### Summarizing and Sequencing

On strips of paper, write sentences based on the events that students have included on their Story Elements chart. Invite students to arrange the events in the order of the story to help summarize the plot.

### Using a Graphic Organizer

Use the T-Chart on page xi to create a two-column chart with the headings: *Dogs are pets. Dogs can work.* For each of the headings, have students give examples of things dogs do and help them record their examples on the chart. If students do not mention sled dogs, remind them that dogs like Wolf are often used for this kind of work. Students can use what they know about Walt and Madge to guess what they would think of making dogs work.

## Read the Selection

Ask students to follow along on page 18 of their books as you play track 5 on the Level Three CD or read aloud lines 1–14. Check students' understanding of the passage.

1. What did Wolf do when he heard Skiff talk?
2. Why does Skiff sit down?
3. Why are Walt and Madge surprised?
4. Why did Madge think Wolf was friendly to Skiff?

Check that students understand key vocabulary in the selection. Encourage students to visualize what is happening. Remind them of Wolf's actions in the first and second parts of the story. What does Wolf do now that is different? Encourage students to suggest why Wolf is acting friendly.

Play CD track 6 or read lines 15–31 on page 18. Check students' comprehension of the passage by using any or all of the following questions.

1. Who touched Wolf's paw?
2. Was the paw soft or hard? What did this show?
3. When Wolf barked, who was shocked? Why?
4. Was this the first time that Skiff had seen Wolf?
5. How did he know Wolf?

Stop and allow students to think about what they have discovered in this section of the story. Encourage them to guess how Walt and Madge feel about Wolf belonging to Miller and then have them read to find the answer.

Read lines 32–66 on page 19 or play track 7 on the CD. Use questions such as those listed below to check understanding.

1. What name did Miller call the dog?
2. How did Miller prove that the dog was his?
3. Where did Miller want to take the dog?
4. Why did Madge and Walt want the dog to stay in California?

Help students summarize and record the information and events on their Story Elements chart. Review key vocabulary. Check to see if any of the predictions that students made about Skiff Miller and Wolf were correct.

## Model a Strategy: Comparing and Contrasting

Make a large Venn diagram on the board. Label one of the circles *Walt and Madge* and the other *Skiff Miller*. Write similarities in the intersection of the two circles on the diagram as you say: "These characters are the same in some ways. They all like the dog. They want the dog to stay with them. They will take good care of the dog."

Write differences in the appropriate portions of the circles as you say: "These characters are different. Walt and Madge live in California. They don't want the dog to work. Skiff Miller lives in Alaska. He wants the dog to work pulling sleds."

Have students suggest other similarities and differences between the main characters and add them to the diagram. Help students make statements that compare and contrast the characters.

## You Can Answer These Questions

This activity can be assigned as classwork or as homework.

| | | | |
|---|---|---|---|
| 1. | c | 6. | c |
| 2. | a | 7. | c |
| 3. | b | 8. | c |
| 4. | b | 9. | b |
| 5. | b | 10. | a |

## Exercises to Help You

### Forming Questions and Answers: *why* and *because*

Write *why?* and *because* on the board. Ask questions beginning with *why* and have volunteers answer them. Write the answers on the board, pointing out the use of *because* in the answers to introduce the reasons. Some questions might be:

Why is Wolf friendly to Skiff?

Why are Walt and Madge surprised when Wolf barks?

Why does Skiff want to take the dog to Alaska?

Encourage students to create more *why* questions for others to answer.

Students can do Exercises A, B, and C on pages 21–23. You may want to arrange students in pairs or groups to complete them as classwork or assign the exercises for homework.

*Exercise A*

Students' sentences will vary. Suggested answers:

1. Skiff Miller sat down on a log.
2. Miller sat down because he was very surprised.
3. Skiff Miller was from Alaska.
4. The dog's paw felt soft.
5. They had never heard Wolf bark before.
6. The dog turned at once.
7. The dog was born in Alaska.
8. The dog grew up in Alaska.

## Exercise B

1. b  Wolf looked at the man's hands.
2. d  Skiff Miller reached out and patted the dog's head.
3. a  Madge said the dog was from Alaska.
4. c  Miller said he had heard the dog bark before.
5. c  Madge suddenly felt scared.
6. a  Skiff Miller's voice sounded angry.
7. d  The dog stared ahead and waited.
8. b  Miller said that the dog was strong.

## Exercise C

1. log
2. licked
3. tongue
4. paws
5. suffer
6. team

## Using the Present Tense: Third Person Singular

Write sentences on the board about the selection using plural present tense forms, such as:

Madge and Walt *want* to keep Wolf.

Skiff's dogs *turn* when he says, "Turn."

Invite volunteers to read the sentences. Then help them change the sentences so they have a singular subject:

Skiff *wants* to keep Wolf too.

Wolf *turns* too.

Write the new sentences on the board, pointing out the *-s* on the verb forms. You may want to exaggerate the */s/* and */z/* sounds as you say the responses.

Ask students to look through page 19 for other examples of the third person singular form of the present tense. As students read the sentences aloud, remind them of the *-s.*

Assign Exercises D, E, and F on pages 23–25.

## Exercise D

1. works
2. pulls
3. listens
4. turns
5. barks
6. likes

When he is in Alaska, Brown *works* hard. He *pulls* a sled through the snow. Brown always *listens* to his owner. When his owner says, "Turn," Brown *turns.* Brown *barks* all the time. He *likes* Alaska very much.

## Exercise E

1. F
2. F
3. T
4. T
5. T
6. F
7. T
8. F

## Exercise F

Students' sentences will vary.

## Sharing with Others

Before students do this activity, have the class brainstorm chores, work, and jobs. Students can include household chores along with jobs and occupational tasks. Then arrange students in pairs or small groups to discuss the work preference questions on page 25.

After students choose one of the topics and write their individual answers, encourage them to work with a partner, reading and helping edit their partner's work.

Compile students' final copies of their writing in a booklet for placement in the class library or for supplementary reading practice. ■

# Wolf

Part Four, pages 26–33

## Warm Up

Use any or all of the activities below.

### Dramatizing

Invite volunteers to role-play the characters in the story. Students can use the dialogues in the story as they dramatize the events or improvise their own dialogues. Guide discussion of how the characters feel and interact with each other.

### Thinking It Over: Think–Pair–Share

Write the following incomplete sentences on the board:

> I lost my ____ so I felt ____. I see it and now I feel ____. I want to
> _____.

Model thinking it over, giving examples of different feelings and actions that might be used to fill the blanks. Then arrange students in pairs to talk about how they want to complete the sentences. Invite pairs to share their responses with the class.

### Using the Illustrations

Ask students to look at the illustration on page 27 and consider how Skiff Miller might be feeling. As a group, discuss why he is angry and what he might want to do in this next part of the story. Help students use details in the illustration, such as his raised fist, on which to base their predictions.

## Read the Selection

Play track 8 on the CD or read aloud lines 1–14 as students follow along on page 26 of their books. Ask questions to check students' comprehension of the passage.

1. Who wanted the dog to go to Alaska and pull sleds?
2. How do you know that Skiff was angry?
3. Why did Skiff raise his fist and walk toward Walt?

Be sure that students understand the key vocabulary in the passage. Invite students to predict what is going to happen between Walt and Skiff.

Play CD track 9 or read lines 15–32 on pages 26–27. Check students' understanding of the passage with questions such as the following.

1. Why did Madge step between the two men?
2. Who wanted to buy the dog?
3. How long had Skiff Miller been looking for the dog?
4. Did he want to sell the dog? Why not?

Help students describe the main problem in the story and the solutions that have been tried by the characters to resolve it.

Play CD track 10 or read lines 33–52 on page 27. Check students' comprehension with any or all of the following questions.

1. Why did Madge think Skiff didn't care about the dog?
2. Who did Madge think should choose where the dog would live?
3. How did Miller describe the dog?
4. Was the dog listening to the people? How do you know?

Students can summarize the problem and events of the selection, and add them to their Story Elements charts. Write the ideas on the board and review vocabulary as needed.

## Model a Strategy: Identifying Problems and Solutions

Say: "Walt and Madge have taken care of the dog for a while. They want to keep the dog in California. Skiff Miller had the dog in Alaska, but it was stolen. He wants to take the dog back to Alaska. So the problem is everyone wants the dog. The characters argue and almost fight. That doesn't solve the problem. Walt and Madge want to buy the dog. But Miller doesn't want to sell it. Now they solve the problem by letting the dog decide. I wonder if the people will be happy with what the dog decides."

Encourage students to think about the two possible choices the dog has, and about how the characters might react.

## Punctuation

Write examples on the board of sentences from the selection that end in a period, question mark, and exclamation point. Read the sentences and invite students to comment on the intonation used in each of the sentences. Explain the use of an exclamation point for emphasis. Students can find and read other examples.

 **You Can Answer These Questions**

You can assign this activity as classwork or as homework.

| | |
|---|---|
| 1. c | 6. b |
| 2. b | 7. a |
| 3. a | 8. c |
| 4. c | 9. b |
| 5. a | 10. a |

**Exercises to Help You**

### Using the Past Tense: Regular Verbs

Ask questions about the selection using regular verbs in the past tense and write the responses on the board. Ask: "What did the dog pull in Alaska? Whom did the dog look at? Who wanted the dog?"

The dog *pulled* a sled.

The dog *looked* at Skiff and Madge.

They all *wanted* the dog.

Point out the *-ed* ending on the verbs. Ask students to look through pages 26–27 for other examples and list the words on the board. Say the words and have students repeat the forms. Guide students to notice and repeat the different pronunciation of the endings /d/, /t/, /əd/.

Assign Exercises A, B, C, and D on pages 29–31. Students can work in pairs or groups to complete the exercises as classwork, or you can assign them for homework.

### Exercise A
Students' sentences will vary. Suggested answers:

1. He was very angry.
2. Madge stepped between the two men.
3. He was very happy.

4. Wolf's real name was Brown.
5. Miller felt sick.
6. Miller looked for Wolf for three years.
7. He watched them.

*Exercise B*

1. d  Walt thought that any dog from Alaska would listen to Miller.
2. c  Skiff Miller stared down at Walt.
3. b  Madge asked Miller if he would sell the dog to them.
4. a  Brown was the best dog Miller ever had.
5. c  When he saw the dog, Miller thought that he was dreaming.
6. a  Brown was a very hard worker.
7. d  The dog's ears were standing straight up.
8. b  Miller said he would do whatever the dog wanted.

*Exercise C*

1. sick         5. worth
2. choose       6. care
3. leader       7. lazy
4. understands  8. earned

*Exercise D*

1. pulled       5. turned
2. listened     6. asked
3. raised       7. worked
4. stepped      8. looked

## Using Subject Pronouns

Write sentences on the board that use each of the subject pronouns. Use gestures as necessary to show the meanings and use of the subject pronouns.

*I* like the dog.

*You* don't care about the dog.

*She* stepped between the two men.

*We* want to buy the dog.

*They* want the dog to stay.

Students can create sentences about themselves and the story characters using the subject pronouns.

Assign Exercises E and F on pages 32–33.

*Exercise E*

1. he    5. they
2. she   6. we
3. I     7. you
4. you   8. it

*Exercise F*
Students' sentences will vary.

## Sharing with Others

Bring in a world map and invite students to locate and identify places they know and places where they have lived. Have the class brainstorm a list of things that they like about these places, such as weather, jobs, activities, people, food, and so on. Then arrange students in pairs or small groups for discussion of the two questions on page 33. Encourage students to explain and give examples of things that they like about their chosen places.

After students choose one of the topics, guide them to use the T-Chart, page xi, to record their ideas before writing by putting the place or country in the left column and what they are going to write about that place or country in the right column.

Prepare a display of students' writing, a world map indicating the places, and photos or pictures of the various places. Encourage students to read each others' work and comment on what they like about the writing. ■

# Wolf

Part Five, pages 34–41

## Warm Up

Use any or all of the activities below.

### Rereading and Reviewing

Ask students to go back to page 27 and reread lines 40–52. Ask students to tell who is going to choose where the dog will go. Then discuss why the dog is going to choose. Point out line 52 and have students explain the meaning of "The dog has earned the right to choose."

### Dramatizing

Encourage volunteers to act out Part Four using the dialogue from pages 26–27. Discuss the gestures and nonverbal behavior that indicate the feelings and emotions of the characters.

### Making Predictions

Write *dog* or draw a dog in the center of the board. Write *Alaska* to the right and *California* to the left of the dog. Ask students where they think the dog will choose to go. Note the responses on the board. Then have students consider how the people will ask the dog where it wants to go. Encourage students to discuss or act out how they would give a dog a choice.

## Read the Selection

Have students follow along on page 34 of their books as you play CD track 11 or read aloud lines 1–16. Ask questions to check understanding of the passage.

1. Who was going to walk away?
2. Why was Skiff going to say good-bye?
3. Where was the dog?
4. What did the dog do as Skiff walked away?

Check that students understand the key vocabulary and the action in the selection. Encourage students to discuss whether this seems to be a fair test for the dog.

Play track 12 on the CD or read lines 17–43 on pages 34–35. Use any or all of the following questions to check students' comprehension.

1. Where did Wolf run first?
2. Where did the dog want Walt to go?
3. Why didn't the people talk to the dog?
4. How did the dog feel? How do you know?
5. When did Wolf lie down?
6. What did Wolf choose?

Guide students in summarizing the events in this final selection. Add the dog's final decision to the Story Elements chart and review key vocabulary. Check to see if any of the predictions that students made about the story were correct.

## Model a Strategy: Drawing Conclusions

Say: "If I think about the ending of the story, I can make some guesses about how the characters feel. Wolf ran down the road after Miller, so I guess that Miller is more important to the dog than Walt and Madge. Miller was going to fight to keep the dog, so I am sure that Miller is very happy about the dog's choice. Walt and Madge wanted to buy the dog, so they are probably disappointed that the dog didn't stay with them."

Students can draw their own conclusions based on the events of the story.

## Apostrophes

Review contractions and have students find examples on pages 34–35. Write the examples on the board and help students tell what the two original words are. Review the use of the apostrophe to indicate letters that are omitted. Contrast with examples of possessive nouns: *Walt's, Miller's*. Ask students to find other examples in the passage.

## You Can Answer These Questions

You can assign this activity as classwork or as homework.

| | |
|---|---|
| 1. c | 6. b |
| 2. b | 7. a |
| 3. c | 8. a |
| 4. a | 9. b |
| 5. b | 10. b |

## Exercises to Help You

### Using Prepositions of Location

Model sentences using prepositions of location as you demonstrate or draw arrows to show the direction of the actions. Write the sentences on the board.

Wolf ran *in front of* Miller.

Miller walked *around* the dog.

The dog ran *toward* Madge.

The man was *at* the curve.

The dog walked *to* Walt.

Wolf lay *on* his side.

Explain that these prepositions help answer the question *Where*. Have students create their own sentences using the prepositions.

Assign Exercises A, B, and C on pages 37–39. You may want to arrange students in pairs or groups to complete the exercises as classwork or assign them for homework.

### Exercise A

Students' sentences will vary. Suggested answers:

1. Skiff Miller began to walk away.
2. The dog heard Skiff Miller say goodbye.
3. He walked around the dog.
4. Walt did not move.
5. Madge did not touch him.
6. Wolf was waiting for Skiff Miller.
7. Wolf ran down the road.

### Exercise B

1. c  The dog was lying on his side.
2. a  Wolf saw the three people shake hands.
3. d  Miller walked around the dog.
4. b  The man was at the end of the road.
5. d  Wolf could not see the man.
6. c  Madge thought that Wolf was staying.
7. a  The dog did not look at the woman and the man.
8. b  He ran faster and faster down the road.

### Exercise C

| | | | |
|---|---|---|---|
| 1. | straight | 4. | teeth |
| 2. | suddenly | 5. | nodded |
| 3. | curve | 6. | minute |

### Using the Past Tense: Irregular Verbs

Write questions about the story using past tense irregular verbs. As students suggest answers, write the responses on the board.

> Did Wolf run after Miller or Walt? He *ran* after Miller.
>
> Did Madge hear Wolf bark? Yes, she *heard* him bark.
>
> What did Wolf see? He *saw* Miller walking away.
>
> Did Wolf go to sleep or get up? He *got* up.
>
> What did Miller say to Walt and Madge? He *said* good-bye.
>
> Why did Walt stand still? He *stood* still so Wolf could choose.

Point out the irregular verb forms. Help students use the irregular forms to talk about the story or themselves.

Assign Exercises D, E, and F on pages 39–41.

*Exercise D*

| | |
|---|---|
| 1. ran | 4. got |
| 2. heard | 5. said |
| 3. saw | 6. stood |

*Exercise E*

1. Wolf lifted his head.
2. Wolf ran down the road.
3. Walt did not move.
4. Miller shook hands with them.
5. Madge did not speak to him.

*Exercise F*
Students' sentences will vary.

### Sharing with Others

Have students work in pairs or small groups as they use the questions on page 41 to discuss their personal reactions to the story.

Have students choose one of the questions. Then give them a copy of the Main Idea chart on page T1 to record their ideas before writing.

Arrange students who have written about the same question in pairs to read together and compare their answers. Invite the pairs to report to the class what similarities and differences they found in their written responses to the story ending. ■

## Answers for Unit 1: Wolf
(The Unit Assessment appears on the following page of this Teacher's Guide.)

1. Skiff Miller said the dog was his.
2. Wolf ran after Skiff.
3. Skiff was angry because Walt wanted to keep the dog.
4. They all thought Wolf had earned the right to choose.
5. Madge and Walt named the dog Wolf.
6. Madge and Walt named the dog Wolf.
7. Skiff Miller said the dog was his.
8. Skiff was angry because Walt wanted to keep the dog.
9. They all thought Wolf had earned the right to choose.
10. Wolf ran after Skiff.

| | | | |
|---|---|---|---|
| 11. | stolen | 19. | likes |
| 12. | sled | 20. | has |
| 13. | growl | 21. | have |
| 14. | prove | 22. | calls |
| 15. | looked | 23. | was |
| 16. | listened | 24. | were |
| 17. | said | 25. | was |
| 18. | heard | | |

**Name** _____ **Date** _____

# Wolf

**A s s e s s m e n t**

**A.** Complete these sentences by drawing lines from the first part to the second part. Write the complete sentences on the lines below, in the same order they happened in the story.

1. Skiff Miller said                    named the dog Wolf.
2. Wolf ran                              earned the right to choose.
3. Skiff was angry                      because Walt wanted to keep the dog.
4. They all thought Wolf had            the dog was his.
5. Madge and Walt                       after Skiff.

6. _____

7. _____

8. _____

9. _____

10. _____

**B.** Complete each sentence by adding the correct word.

**stolen          growl          sled          prove**

11. Wolf was _____ from Skiff Miller in Alaska.

12. A dog team can pull a _____.

13. If a dog is not friendly, it will _____.

14. "It's my dog. I can _____ it," said Skiff.

**C.** Fill in each blank using the past tense of the verbs in parentheses.

15. The dog _____ at Madge. (look)

16. Wolf's ears were straight up. He _____ carefully. (listen)

17. Mr. Miller _____ good-bye to Madge and Walt. (say)

18. They _____ Wolf bark. (hear)

**D.** Fill in each blank using the present tense of the verbs in parentheses.

19. Wolf _____ to work. (like)

20. Skiff Miller _____ long hair. (have)

21. Walt and Madge _____ a fence around the house. (have)

22. Skiff _____ the dog Brown. (call)

**E.** Fill in each blank using *was* or *were*.

23. The dog _____ lost and hungry.

24. Walt and Madge _____ glad to help the dog.

25. Skiff Miller _____ going back to Alaska with the dog.

# Crucita
pages 43–75

# Planning Guide

## Part 1
pages 43–51

Using a map

Word mapping

Using a graphic organizer

Previewing the story

Guessing multiple meanings from context

Using conventions of print

Using plurals of nouns

Using adjectives

## Part 2
pages 52–59

Making a story map

Relating to prior knowledge

Identifying cause and effect

Punctuation

Using the past tense: irregular verbs

Forming questions: *who*

## Part 3
pages 60–67

Summarizing

Thinking back

Using illustrations

Giving a personal reaction

Using possessive nouns

Using the past tense: irregular verbs

## Part 4
pages 68–75

Summarizing and making inferences

Drawing conclusions

Using subject pronouns

Forming questions: past tense: *where*

# Vocabulary

## Story Words

to afford
to arrive
to bump
to climb
to destroy
to join
to joke
to leak
to listen
to realize
to remember
to twist

artist
crash
hail
idea
journey
ledge
middle
squirrel

blind
famous
huge
narrow
several
trapped

## Words Relating to Village Life

to gather

child
mule
parent
wagon

## Words Relating to Religion

to pray

candle
church

## Idioms

to call on

all at once
all right
at first
at once
every so often
in a hurry
so far

# Crucita

pages 43-75

## Story Synopsis

Crucita Valdéz lived in a small village in New Mexico called San Eliso. Although Crucita was partially blind and not considered beautiful, she was a helpful and thoughtful girl. As she grew older, she had mysterious dreams and premonitions that foretold events in the future. She was able to help rescue some lost boys, and she helped the villagers avoid losing their crops to a destructive hailstorm. Crucita helped in the local church, an old structure that needed to be replaced. On a trip to Santa Fe, Crucita met an artist who drew her picture and listened to her talk about the village and church. Years later she received a stained glass window from the artist, and money to help the villagers build a new church. The woman pictured in the stained glass window looked like Crucita.

## About the Author

Manuela Williams Crosno (1905–1997) lived most of her life in Las Cruces, New Mexico. The settings of many of her stories are in New Mexico, specifically in the areas around Santa Fe, Albuquerque, and Taos. Crosno's interest in Hispanic culture was reflected in the subject matter of many of those stories. Crosno was an English teacher and won a statewide essay contest with an essay entitled "Why I Teach School." In addition to being a teacher and writer, she was also an accomplished poet, artist, and illustrator.

Bring in a map of the United States and have students find New Mexico and some of its major cities. Encourage students to share any information they know about the area. You may want to have students look through resource materials for information about New Mexico. Prepare a chart to guide students' research.

Students may want to make or collect pictures that show different aspects of New Mexico and the cultural groups that live there. If students want to, invite them to create a collage or bulletin board display.

New Mexico

Major Cities

Climate

Cultures

Land Features

Housing

# Introducing the Story

Have students look at the opening illustration on page 42. Guide discussion of the characters and setting pictured. Encourage students to point out and comment on details in the picture. Use the questions on page 43 to help focus the discussion.

*Note:* Remind students that there are no "right" answers to these questions; they are making guesses about the story, and they will find out if their guesses are correct as they read. Guide students to point out details from the picture that support their guesses. Accept all reasonable answers.

## Vocabulary Option

Write the word *village* on the board and ask students to brainstorm words and phrases they associate with it. List students' ideas as they are suggested. Students can use the illustration on page 43 for ideas, or you can ask questions to guide the activity: Who lives in a village? What type of work do people do? What buildings are in villages? You may want to suggest some of the key vocabulary words from the story to add to the list.

## Writing Option

Students can compose a description of the village setting or a character sketch of one of the characters from the illustration. Encourage them to think of using all their senses as they discuss their descriptions with a partner. What would you (or the character) hear, see, and smell in the village? How does the weather make you (or the character) feel? Suggest that students list their ideas before writing.

# Crucita

**Part One, pages 43–51**

## Warm Up

Use any or all of the activities below.

### Using a Map

Bring in a map of North America. Help students locate Mexico, the Rio Grande, Santa Fe, and Mexico City. Guide discussion of map symbols and keys that indicate geographical features. Students can share what they may know about the climate and culture of the people living in these areas.

### Word Mapping

As a group, begin a word map for *village* to help students classify words. Start with some of the words and phrases that students suggested in the Vocabulary Option. Guide students to arrange words into categories for the mapping.

### Using a Graphic Organizer

Students can compare a village with a large city. Bring in one or more pictures of Mexico City, or any other large city, and invite students to suggest how it is similar to and different from the village pictured on page 42. Distribute copies of the Venn diagram on page x and help students label the left side *village* (or *San Eliso*) and the right side *large city* (or *Mexico City*). Help students write the differences in the correct circle and the similarities in the overlapping space.

## Previewing the Story

Explain to students that many people in New Mexico speak Spanish. Encourage students to share Spanish names that they know. Introduce the names of the characters in the story and help students pronounce the names (Crucita Valdéz: croo-SEE-tah vahl-DAYS; Isabella: ee-sah-BEL-lah; Rosita: rrrrow-SEE-tah; Filiberto: fee-lee-BEAR-toe). Have students look for the names on pages 44–45.

## Read the Selection

Students can follow along on page 44 of their books as you read lines 1–18 aloud or play track 13 on the CD. Check understanding of the passage by asking any or all of the following questions.

1. Where did Crucita live?
2. Who were Isabella and Rosita?
3. What did Crucita look like?
4. Was Crucita a good or bad child? How do you know?

Check students' understanding of key vocabulary. Explain that it is not necessary to know the meaning of every word to get the general meaning of a passage.

Play CD track 14 or read lines 19–35 on pages 44–45. Check for understanding, using any or all of the following questions.

1. Where was the church in town?
2. Why did the people want a new church?
3. Who realized that Crucita was almost blind?

After reading the passage, help students summarize the story and describe the main character. As students retell the important information, list the ideas on the board and review key vocabulary.

## Model a Strategy: Guessing Multiple Meanings from Context

Say: "On page 45, line 28, I read the name Sister Mary Olivia. The word *sister* is capitalized here. But on page 44, line 3, the word *sisters* is not capitalized. I know that Rosita and Isabella are part of Crucita's family. They are her sisters. Mary Olivia is not part of Crucita's family. Maybe Sister is part of Mary Olivia's name. She works in the church. Maybe *Sister* refers to a woman who works in the church."

## Using Conventions of Print

Point out the accent mark used in the Spanish name on line 1 of the story. Elicit from students any other Spanish names or words they know that have accent marks and write them on the board.

# **Y**ou Can Answer These Questions

Students can complete the comprehension activity in class or as homework.

| | | | |
|---|---|---|---|
| 1. | c | 6. | c |
| 2. | c | 7. | b |
| 3. | b | 8. | b |
| 4. | a | 9. | a |
| 5. | b | 10. | a |

# **E**xercises to Help You

## Using Plurals of Nouns

Write a list of singular nouns used in the story. Invite students to use the words in sentences.

| | |
|---|---|
| sister | word |
| eye | parent |

Then model using the plural forms in sentences. Invite volunteers to suggest how to spell the plural forms. Write the forms on the board. Point out the *-s*, which is usually used for plurals. Depending on the level of the class, you may want to explain plurals of nouns that end in consonant *-y,* using *party/parties* as an example. Students can look back through pages 44–45 for examples of plural nouns.

Ask students to complete Exercises A, B, and C on pages 47–49. Students may work in pairs or groups to complete the exercises or work on them individually for homework.

### *Exercise A*

Students' sentences will vary. Suggested answers:

1. Crucita Valdéz lived in a small village.
2. Crucita had two sisters.
3. Crucita was not beautiful.
4. Crucita walked in a very strange way.
5. He did not think Crucita could hear his words.
6. The church was the biggest building in the village.
7. The people of San Eliso wanted a new church.
8. Sister Mary found out that Crucita could hardly see.

### *Exercise B*

1. d  Crucita Valdéz had large black eyes.
2. c  One day Crucita was sitting on the steps of her house.
3. a  Filiberto did not think that Crucita could hear his words.
4. b  He said that she was a wonderful child.
5. b  The church was the meeting place for the villagers.
6. c  It was very important to the people of San Eliso.
7. d  Cold winds blew through the walls.
8. a  Sister Mary was showing Crucita some words in a book.

### Exercise C

| | | | |
|---|---|---|---|
| 1. | church | 4. | prayed |
| 2. | child | 5. | parents |
| 3. | middle | 6. | blind |

## Using Adjectives

Write several adjectives and names of characters and places from the story on the board:

| | |
|---|---|
| kind | San Eliso |
| small | church |
| old | Crucita |

Guide students to describe the characters and setting in the story using these adjectives. Encourage students to suggest more than one sentence for each adjective. For example:

Crucita is kind.
Crucita is a kind girl.

San Eliso is small.
San Eliso is a small village.

The church is old.
It is an old church.

Write students' suggestions on the board. Ask them to compare the two sentences. Point out the placement of the adjective before the noun in the second sentence. Students can look back through the selection for other sentences with adjectives used in both patterns.

Assign Exercises D, E, and F on pages 49–51.

### Exercise D
**Part A**

1. T  2. F  3. F  4. F  5. T

### Exercise D
**Part B**
The structure of students' sentences may vary.

a. The village was called San Eliso.
b. Crucita could not see very well.
c. The people of the village wanted a new church.

### Exercise E
**Part A**

| | | | |
|---|---|---|---|
| 1. | small | 4. | wonderful |
| 2. | new | 5. | beautiful |
| 3. | strange | | |

### Exercise E
**Part B**
Students' sentences will vary.

### Exercise F
Students' sentences will vary.

## Sharing with Others

Before students work in pairs or small groups to discuss the questions on page 51, you may want to read the questions with the class. Remind students of what they know about Crucita's eyes. Encourage them to think of people and events from their own experience to support their responses.

After students decide on one of the questions, give them a graphic organizer such as the Main Idea chart, page T1, to record their ideas before actually writing.

Invite students to share their writing by reading it aloud. Students can compare their responses and discuss differences. Alternatively, make an exhibit of the writing on a bulletin board or on a table for students to look through. ■

# Crucita

Part Two, pages 52-59

## Warm Up

Use any or all of the activities below.

### Summarizing:
### Making a Story Map

Guide students in identifying and describing the main character and setting of the story. Encourage students to give details to support their ideas. As a class, begin creating a story map using the Story Elements chart on page xii. Have students continue to fill in the information on their own or in pairs. Encourage students to add events as they read the rest of the story.

### Relating to Prior
### Knowledge: Dreams

Ask students about dreams: What are dreams? When do people dream? Are dreams real? Can dreams tell the future? Record students' ideas on the board. Students can share any stories or beliefs they have about dreams.

### Brainstorming: Emergencies

Draw or bring in a Red Cross or first aid kit and guide discussion of emergency situations. Explain to students that they are going to read about an emergency in the next section of the story. Have students suggest different types of emergencies and how to handle them. Be sure to include getting lost and minor injuries such as sprained or twisted ankles. Write words and phrases that students suggest on the board.

## Read the Selection

Play track 15 on the CD or read aloud lines 1–22 as students follow along on page 52 of their books. Use questions such as the ones below to check students' understanding of the passage.

1. Whom did Crucita dream about?
2. What happened in her dream?
3. Why did some men come to Crucita's house?
4. How long had Ricardo and Hermano been lost?

Check that students understand key vocabulary in the selection. Encourage students to consider if Crucita seems to be a happy or lonely person. Then let students suggest what they think will happen to the two lost boys.

Play CD track 16 or read lines 23–43 on pages 52–53. Check students' comprehension of the passage by using any or all of the following questions.

1. How did Crucita know where to find the boys?
2. Where did the men find the boys?
3. How did the boys get hurt?
4. Who saved the boys?

Encourage volunteers to summarize the events of the selection. Write the key ideas on the board and review key vocabulary. Ask students what they have learned about Crucita. How is she special?

## Model a Strategy:
### Identifying Cause and Effect

Say: "When I read a story, sometimes I need to stop and think about what has happened and why it happened. In this part of the story, I read that Crucita was worried. Why was she worried? She was worried because of a strange dream. The dream caused her to become worried."

Create a T-Chart on the board, labeling the headings *Why* (*Cause*) and *What* (*Effect*). Demonstrate how to fill in the causes and the effects. Distribute copies of the T-Chart on page xi. Encourage students to list events from the story in the *What* column: the men came to the house, the boys got hurt, the boys were saved. Have them think about the causes of these events and fill in the *Why* column.

### Punctuation

Guide students to notice the use of exclamation marks and question marks in the conversations. Model the sentences and guide discussion of what the punctuation marks mean to the reader. Help students read the sentences aloud using appropriate intonation. You may also point out the tilde over the *n* in the word *Señor*. Explain that this makes the *n* sound like the first *n* in the word *onion*.

## You Can Answer These Questions

Students may do this activity as classwork or as homework.

| | | | |
|---|---|---|---|
| 1. | b | 6. | b |
| 2. | c | 7. | c |
| 3. | a | 8. | a |
| 4. | c | 9. | b |
| 5. | a | 10. | c |

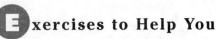

## Exercises to Help You

### Using the Past Tense: Irregular Verbs

Ask questions about the story to elicit examples of irregular verbs in the past tense. For example: From where did the birds eat? (They ate from Crucita's hand.) Write the verbs from the questions and the answers on the board. Help students use the following verbs.

| | | | |
|---|---|---|---|
| eat | ate | meet | met |
| run | ran | do | did |
| wake | woke | break | broke |
| ride | rode | bring | brought |

Guide students to comment on the irregular forms and then to ask and answer additional questions about the story and themselves using the verbs.

Assign Exercises A, B, and C on pages 55–57. Students can work in pairs or groups to complete the exercises as classwork, or you can assign them for homework.

*Exercise A*

Students' sentences will vary. Suggested answers:

1. Crucita loved to play in the forest.
2. The animals were Crucita's friends.
3. Crucita looked worried because she had a strange dream.
4. Crucita dreamed that Ricardo and Hermano were trapped on the mountain.
5. The men were looking for Ricardo and Hermano.
6. The men rode toward the mountain.
7. The rope broke.
8. Crucita saved the boys.

*Exercise B*

1. b  Crucita could not see well.
2. d  Ricardo and Hermano were very wild.
3. a  Señor Valdéz believed that the boys were safe.
4. c  The men rode along the side of the river.
5. c  Señor Valdéz told the men about Crucita's dream.
6. d  She said the boys were near the top of a mountain.
7. a  The men got to the mountain just before dark.
8. b  The boys fell and landed on the path.

*Exercise C*

1. squirrels
2. all right
3. remember
4. climbed
5. ledge
6. narrow

**Forming Questions: *who***

Write sentences on the board about characters in the story. Model asking a *who* question based on the sentence. Then write the question.

> Crucita had a dream.
> *Who* had a dream?
>
> Señor Valdéz talked to the men.
> *Who* talked to the men?
>
> Ricardo and Hermano were lost.
> *Who* was lost?

Help students explain how the questions are formed from the sentences. Point out that the question word *who* uses a singular verb form.

Assign Exercises D, E, and F on pages 57–59.

*Exercise D*

1. ate
2. woke
3. rode
4. met
5. did
6. brought
7. broke

*Exercise E*

1. Who could not see well?
2. Who ran to Crucita when she called?
3. Who were Ricardo and Hermano?
4. Who told Crucita not to worry?
5. Who rode up to the house that afternoon?
6. Who told them what happened?
7. Who thanked Señor Valdéz?

*Exercise F*
Students' sentences will vary.

## Sharing with Others

Before students discuss the answers to the questions on page 59 in pairs or small groups, guide discussion of dreams and nightmares. Guide students to talk about what they know or have heard about dreams. Help students make guesses about Ricardo's and Hermano's future mountain trips based on what they read in the selection. Encourage students to give details and examples to support their opinions.

Students should choose one of the questions to answer in writing. They can use the Main Idea chart, page T1, to record their ideas before writing.

If students are interested, have them create drawings or collages to illustrate their writing. Display students' work for others to read and discuss. ■

# Crucita

**Part Three, pages 60–67**

## Warm Up

Use any or all of the activities below.

### Summarizing

Ask students to think back to what they have read about Crucita. Invite them to suggest words that describe Crucita. Write the words or phrases on the board. Encourage students to describe or summarize how the character overcomes weak points or uses her good traits to help others. Students can discuss what traits they admire about Crucita.

### Thinking Back

On pieces of paper, write some possible reactions of characters in the story to Crucita. Invite volunteers to select a paper, read it aloud, and guess what character might have said it. For example: Thank you for saving me. Hermano and I were so scared on the mountain. (Ricardo) My daughter's dream was true. She is a very special person. (Señor Valdéz) You may want to have students write their own character reactions for others in the class to guess.

### Using Illustrations

As students look at the picture on page 61, guide discussion of the scene. Have students talk about what the people are doing. Help students make predictions about the next selection. For example, say: "Crucita has helped many people in the story. I wonder if she will help with the crops and farms. How could she help?" List students' ideas on the board.

### Brainstorming

Ask students to suggest words and phrases that they associate with farming. Make a list of the words as students suggest them, including key vocabulary. Encourage students to share any experiences they have had with farming or gardening.

## Read the Selection

Ask students to follow along on page 60 of their books as you play track 17 on the Level Three CD or read aloud lines 1–24. Check students' understanding of the passage with these questions.

1. When did Crucita think the family should plant the crops?
2. Why was her father surprised?
3. What did the neighbor remember about Crucita?

Check that students understand key vocabulary in the selection. Take a poll to see if students would follow Crucita's suggestion. Encourage students to explain why they would or would not listen to Crucita.

Play CD track 18 or read lines 25–47 on pages 60–61. Check comprehension of the passage by using any or all of the following questions.

1. How did the crops grow that year?
2. What did Isabella and Rosita see in the sky?
3. What fell with the rain?
4. Why were the farmers glad they had planted early?

Stop and allow students to think about what happened in this selection. Encourage them to guess what the people in the village think about Crucita now. Help students summarize and record the information and events on their Story Elements chart. Review key vocabulary.

**Model a Strategy: Giving a Personal Reaction**

Encourage students to think back about the events in this selection. After students summarize the events, say: "The farmers were glad they had gathered the crops. The storm was terrible, but later there was a beautiful rainbow in the sky. What did you think of this?"

Students can give their own reactions to the contrasting weather conditions or give their own thoughts on Crucita's character and role in the village. Record students' ideas on the board. Help the class summarize their personal reactions.

## Y ou Can Answer These Questions

This activity can be assigned as classwork or as homework.

| | | | |
|---|---|---|---|
| 1. | c | 6. | c |
| 2. | b | 7. | b |
| 3. | c | 8. | c |
| 4. | a | 9. | c |
| 5. | a | 10. | a |

## E xercises to Help You

**Using Possessive Nouns**

Write these sentences on the board:

Señor Valdéz is the father of Crucita.
Señor Valdéz is Crucita's father.

Guide students to notice the differences between the two sentences. Point out the *'s* used to indicate possession. Write other sentences and invite students to suggest ways to rewrite the sentences using possessive nouns.

The mother of Crucita helped plant the crops.

The neighbor of Ricardo came to the house.

Students can create their own sentences about themselves or the characters in the story using possessives.

Students can do Exercises A, B, and C on pages 63–65. You may want to arrange students in pairs or groups to complete the exercises as classwork, or you can assign them for homework.

*Exercise A*
Students' sentences will vary. Suggested answers:

1. Crucita told her parents to plant the crops soon.
2. The next week Señor Valdéz began to plant the crops.
3. A neighbor asked Señor Valdéz why he was planting so early.
4. He began to plant his crops the next day.
5. Everything grew very well that year.
6. It rained very hard.
7. The hail broke some windows in the house.
8. They saw a beautiful rainbow in the sky.

### Exercise B

1. d   Crucita was eating dinner with her parents.
2. a   Her mother wanted to know why they should plant so early that year.
3. b   The neighbor had heard about Crucita's dream.
4. c   He remembered how Crucita saved Ricardo and Hermano.
5. c   Señor Valdéz was sitting in the living room with his wife.
6. a   Everyone ran to the window and looked outside.
7. d   The pieces of hail crashed down everywhere.
8. b   When the storm was over, the sun came out.

### Exercise C

1. idea
2. listen
3. joking
4. huge
5. crash
6. at first

## Using the Past Tense: Irregular Verbs

Write these verbs on the board:

tell   grow   come   think   begin

Ask questions based on the story and have students look back through the selection for the sentence that answers the question. Have volunteers write the answers next to the verbs. For example:

What *did* Señor Valdéz *tell* his neighbor?
He *told* him what Crucita had said.

Point out the irregular verb forms. Have students practice asking and answering questions in the past tense using the verbs from the list.

Assign Exercises D, E, and F on pages 65–67.

### Exercise D

1. told
2. thought
3. grew
4. came
5. began

### Exercise E

1. It was a day in the spring.
2. The crops came up early.
3. Crucita's sisters ran into the house.
4. They saw a beautiful rainbow.
5. The terrible storm was suddenly over. (Other sentences are possible; the word *suddenly* can be put in several different places in the sentence.)

### Exercise F

Students' sentences will vary.

## Sharing with Others

Read the questions on page 67 together before arranging students in pairs or small groups for discussion.

Have students choose one of the questions to write about. Distribute copies of the Main Idea chart on page T1 for students to record their ideas before writing. After students write their individual answers, encourage them to work with partners, reading and helping edit each others' work. Invite students to draw pictures to illustrate their ideas.

Display students' work on a bulletin board or on a table for students to read in their free time. ■

# Crucita

## Warm Up

Use any or all of the activities below.

### Summarizing and Making Inferences

Ask students to look back at the Story Elements chart and retell what they know about Crucita. As students talk about Crucita, guide them to make generalizations about her by asking how Crucita might act in the classroom. Would she be quiet or would she talk a lot? Would she enjoy being in the classroom or would she rather be outside? Students can look back through the story for details to support their inferences.

## Read the Selection

Have students follow along on page 68 of their books as you play CD track 19 or read aloud lines 1–21. Ask questions to check understanding of the passage.

1.  How did Crucita help in the church?
2.  Whom did Crucita help?
3.  Where did Crucita want to go?
4.  How did they travel to Santa Fe?

Check that students understand key vocabulary and the information in the selection. Encourage students to comment on the character of Crucita and make predictions about what she will do in Santa Fe.

Play CD track 20 or read lines 22–51 on pages 68–69. Use any or all of the following questions to check students' comprehension.

1.  Where did Crucita want to walk in Santa Fe?
2.  Whom did she bump into?
3.  Where is the artist from? Whom did he want to draw?
4.  What did Crucita tell the artist about?

Ask students if they think anything important happened during the trip to Santa Fe. Students can make predictions before you complete the reading of lines 52–67 on page 69 or play CD track 21. Check understanding with questions.

1.  How many years went by?
2.  What did people call Crucita? Was that a good name for her? Why?
3.  What was the artist sending?
4.  What was she to do with the money and the stained glass window?
5.  What did people say about the window?

You may want to have students summarize the events in this final selection and add notes about the conclusion to their Story Elements chart. Have students check to see if any of the predictions that they made about the story were correct. Review key vocabulary.

### Model a Strategy: Drawing Conclusions

Say: "Sometimes the author wants the reader to think about what happened. There is something strange here. In the beginning of the story, Crucita's grandfather said she was not beautiful, but now everybody in the village says Crucita is beautiful. She is still almost blind. She still walks very slowly and bumps into people. Why do the people say she is beautiful?"

Encourage students to draw their own conclusions using events and information from the story to support their conclusions.

## You Can Answer These Questions

You can assign this activity as classwork or as homework.

| | | | |
|---|---|---|---|
| 1. | c | 6. | c |
| 2. | c | 7. | b |
| 3. | a | 8. | a |
| 4. | b | 9. | a |
| 5. | b | 10. | c |

## Exercises to Help You

### Using Subject Pronouns

Write these subject pronouns on the board:

I   you   he   she   we   you   they

Ask questions about people in the room and have students respond with the proper subject pronoun. If needed, point to the person or people you are asking about to help clarify the subject of the sentence.

Where are you from? (*I* am from...)

What am I doing? (*You* are...)

Does Miguel live in Boston or...? (*He* lives in...)

Peter, where do you and Ivan study? (*We* study at...)

Do Maria and I like this story? (Yes, *you* do.)

How do Mark and Tung come to school? (*They* come...)

Explain that subject pronouns are used to replace people's names and to tell who is doing the action. Have students look back through the selection on pages 68–69 for examples of the subject pronouns. Guide them to identify who the subject is in each of the sentences.

Assign Exercises A, B, C, and D on pages 71–74. You may want to arrange students in pairs or groups to complete the exercises as classwork or assign them for homework.

### Exercise A

Students' sentences will vary. Suggested answers:

1. Sister Mary Olivia asked Crucita if she would help at the church.
2. Crucita said, "Yes, I would like to help."
3. Crucita planted corn, beans, and grapes in the garden.
4. The artist was drawing pictures of the Plaza.
5. The man worked for a long time.
6. Crucita told him about the village of San Eliso.
7. The letter asked the villagers to build a new church.
8. The window was made of stained glass.

### Exercise B

1. d   Crucita said that she was glad to help.
2. c   She kept the church clean.
3. a   Over the years many people visited the garden.
4. b   Crucita had a warm smile for everyone.
5. c   Crucita played with the children who came to visit her.
6. d   Sister Mary Olivia and Father Isidro went into some shops.
7. a   One window was made by the artist from Mexico City.
8. b   The people thought that the face was very beautiful.

### Exercise C

| | | | |
|---|---|---|---|
| 1. | candle | 5. | several |
| 2. | at once | 6. | joined |
| 3. | wagon | 7. | arrived |
| 4. | mules | 8. | famous |

### Exercise D

| 1. | he | 3. | you | 5. | it | 7. | we |
|---|---|---|---|---|---|---|---|
| 2. | I | 4. | she | 6. | they | 8. | you |

## Forming Questions
## Past Tense: *where*

Write on the board:

> Crucita worked at the church.
>
> *Where did* Crucita work?

Guide students to compare and contrast the question and answer. Point out the word *where* and the use of *did* in the question. Explain that when *did* is used in the question, the past tense ending (*-ed*) is dropped from the verb. Write several other sentences about locations on the board and invite students to create *where* questions.

> Sister Mary Olivia and Crucita traveled to Santa Fe.
>
> The artist lived in Mexico City.
>
> Crucita walked around the Plaza.

Assign Exercises E and F on pages 74–75.

### Exercise E

1. Where did Crucita plant the garden?
2. Where did Crucita want to go?
3. Where did the wagon stop?
4. Where did Crucita want to walk?
5. Where did the artist come from?

### Exercise F
Students' sentences will vary.

## Sharing with Others

Have students work in pairs or small groups as they discuss their personal opinions about the conclusion of the story by answering the questions on page 75. Encourage students to use details from the story to support their ideas.

Have students choose which question they want to write about. They can organize their ideas using a copy of the T-Chart, page xi, to record their ideas and supporting details before writing.

Arrange students' writing on the wall or on a bulletin board to share with the class. ■

# Answers for Unit 2: Crucita
(The Unit Assessment appears on the following page of this Teacher's Guide.)

1. Sister Mary Olivia realized that Crucita could hardly see.
2. The artist sent Crucita a stained glass window.
3. The men planted their crops early because of Crucita.
4. Crucita saved the boys who were lost.
5. Sister Mary Olivia realized that Crucita could hardly see.
6. Crucita saved the boys who were lost.
7. The men planted their crops early because of Crucita.
8. The artist sent Crucita a stained glass window.

9. twisted
10. parents
11. journey
12. artist
13. destroyed
14. came
15. brought
16. rode
17. told

18. They
19. I
20. You

21. Who was lost?
22. Where did they use the new stained glass window?

# Crucita

**A s s e s s m e n t**

**A.** Complete these sentences by drawing lines from the first part to the second part. Write the complete sentences on the lines below, in the same order they happened in the story.

1. Sister Mary Olivia realized that    because of Crucita.
2. The artist sent Crucita    the boys who were lost.
3. The men planted their crops early    a stained glass window.
4. Crucita saved    Crucita could hardly see.

5. _____

6. _____

7. _____

8. _____

**B.** Complete each sentence by adding the correct word.

artist    parents    twisted    destroyed    journey

9. Ricardo was hurt. He had _____ his ankle.

10. The _____ and children all worked to plant the crops.

11. It was a long _____ from San Eliso to Santa Fe.

12. The _____ painted a beautiful picture of Crucita.

13. The storm and hail _____ many plants.

**C.** Fill in each blank using the past tense of the verb in parentheses.

14. Some villagers _____ to see Crucita. (come)

15. They _____ some candles to burn in the church. (bring)

16. Who _____ in the wagon with Crucita? (ride)

17. Sister Mary Olivia _____ many people the story of Crucita. (tell)

**D.** Fill in each blank using one of the pronouns.

I    you    he    she    we    they

18. When did Isabella and Rosita see the rainbow? _____ saw it after the storm.

19. Crucita said, "_____ am going to walk around the Plaza."

20. The grandfather said to Crucita, "_____ are a wonderful child."

**E.** Change each statement to a question.

21. Ricardo was lost. Who _____?

22. They used the stained glass window in the new church. Where _____?

# The Last Leaf

pages 7 7 – 1 0 9

# Planning Guide

## Part 1
### pages 77–85

Using a map

Word mapping

Classifying

Using a graphic organizer

Using conventions of print

Using modal verbs

Forming past tense questions

## Part 2
### pages 86–93

Sequencing and summarizing

Visualizing a story

Understanding time relationships

Using the past tense: irregular verbs

Using prenominal adjectives and indefinite articles

Predicting outcomes

## Part 3
### pages 94–101

Finding the main idea

Using a graphic organizer

Using an illustration

Using *There is/ There are/There was/ There were*

Identifying adverbs

## Part 4
### pages 102–109

Summarizing and using an illustration

Asking reader-generated questions

Comparing and contrasting with a graphic organizer

Using the past tense: irregular verbs

Using prepositions

# Vocabulary

| Story Words | Words Relating to Living Spaces | Words Relating to Illness | Idioms |
|---|---|---|---|
| to draw | alley | to breathe | to turn off |
| to float | apartment | to cough | |
| to howl | desk | to improve | as soon as |
| to shine | rent | | at last |
| to soak | shade | pillow | day after day |
| to tap | | | never mind |
| | downstairs | ill | now and then |
| art | | strong | of course |
| artist | | weak | |
| brick | | | |
| danger | | | |
| ladder | | | |
| leaf | | | |
| moment | | | |
| taxi | | | |
| vacation | | | |
| vine | | | |
| | | | |
| comfortable | | | |
| foolish | | | |

# The Last Leaf

pages 77-109

## Story Synopsis

Joanna lives in Greenwich Village with her friend Sue. Joanna, Sue, and their neighbor Mr. Behrman are all artists. Joanna becomes quite ill with pneumonia and believes that she will die when the last of eight leaves falls from the vine on the brick wall across from her window. Neither the doctor nor Sue can convince her that she will live. Sue tells Mr. Behrman about Joanna's belief, and after the last leaf has fallen, he goes out at night in the cold, rain, and snow to paint on the brick wall a realistic picture of the last leaf, showing it still attached to the vine. Joanna sees that the "last" leaf does not fall, and slowly she recovers. When Joanna is stronger, Sue tells her that Mr. Behrman painted the leaf so that she would live. Mr. Behrman, however, dies from the pneumonia that he contracted after painting in the cold.

## About the Author

William Sydney Porter, known by the pen name O. Henry, is one of the most popular writers of short stories in America. He was born in Greensboro, North Carolina, in 1862. He later moved to New York City, the setting of many of his 300 short stories. O. Henry stories always have an unexpected twist in the plot or a surprise ending. He died in 1910.

Bring in a picture of O. Henry or some reference books in which students can find a picture of the author. Encourage students to talk about the picture by asking questions: What does he look like? Where do you think he is? Is he young or old?

Have students use a map to find O. Henry's birthplace and New York City.

Prepare a chart such as the one here and distribute copies to students. Have them fill in the key information on the chart as you read the paragraph about O. Henry aloud.

| Author's Real Name | |
| --- | --- |
| Author's Pen Name | |
| Born | |
| Died | |
| Stories Known For | |

# Introducing the Story

Have students looks at the opening illustration on page 76. Guide discussion of the characters and setting pictured. Encourage students to point out and comment on details in the picture. Use the questions on page 77 to help focus the discussion. You may also want to use the question below for further discussion of the picture.

- Read the title of the story. Notice the large leaf in the center of the picture. What importance do you think the leaf will have in the story?

*Note:* Students will probably suggest a variety of answers to these questions. Do not stress only one "right" answer at this stage. Allow students to support their answers with details from the picture, and accept any answer that can be logically supported. Point out that they will find out if their predictions are accurate as they work through the story.

## Vocabulary Option

Have students predict from the picture some key vocabulary words that will probably come up in the story. List the words on the board or on chart paper. Add new words to the list as students read through the story.

## Writing Option

At this point, you may want students to work in groups or as a class to write out a simple story or character study based only on the picture. Post the story on the classroom wall and compare and contrast the two stories after the unit is finished.

## Art Appreciation Option

Ask students to look at the picture as a work of art. Have them say if they like it or dislike it and why. You may want to bring into the discussion ideas and concepts such as realistic representation, form, balance, perspective, shading, collage effect, and so forth.

# The Last Leaf

Part One, pages 77-85

## Warm Up

Do any or all of the following activities.

### Using a Map

Have students locate New York state, New York City, and, if possible, Greenwich Village. Help students use the map key to determine how far away they live from New York City. Encourage students to share any experiences they have had or information they know about New York City.

### Word Mapping

Write the word *sickness* on the board and begin a word map, eliciting from students words associated with being sick. You may want to introduce words such as *breathe, cough,* and *weak*. Students can copy the map from the board and add new words as they learn them.

### Classifying

Write the names of the four seasons on the board. Elicit from students descriptive words to put under each category. Focus especially on words that describe winter.

## Read the Selection

Have students follow along in their books on page 78 as you play track 22 on the CD or read lines 1–15 aloud. You may want to stop at this point to check for understanding. Ask any or all of the following questions. Students may answer individually or in groups.

1. Are Joanna and Sue sisters or friends?
2. Where do they live? What do they do?
3. Who gets sick?

Check understanding of key vocabulary. Help students realize that it is not necessary to know the meaning of every word to get the general meaning of a passage.

Play CD track 23 or read lines 16–28 on pages 78–79. Check for understanding using any or all of the following questions.

1. Who came to see Joanna and Sue?
2. What is wrong with Joanna?
3. What does the doctor suggest that Joanna do?

At this point, help students make an oral summary of the story so far. As they summarize, write the key ideas on the board and review key vocabulary.

### Model a Strategy: Using a Story Elements Graphic Organizer

Distribute copies of the Story Elements chart, page xii. Say: "When I'm reading a story, I know I have to remember information. Some important things to remember are whom the story is about, where the story happens, and what the problem in the story is."

Have students work in pairs or groups to fill in the first four boxes (title, setting, characters, problem) for the story. Encourage them to complete the chart as they read the rest of the story.

## Using Conventions of Print

Draw students' attention to the use of dark type (**boldface**) to indicate important vocabulary. Point out the footnote format for the definition of *pneumonia* on page 78. Draw students' attention to the use of italics to indicate a change in emphasis and intonation in spoken lines (*want, believe*) on page 79. Read those sentences aloud, using emphatic intonation.

## **Y**ou Can Answer These Questions

Students can do the comprehension activity in class or as homework.

| | | | |
|---|---|---|---|
| 1. | c | 6. | c |
| 2. | a | 7. | a |
| 3. | b | 8. | c |
| 4. | b | 9. | b |
| 5. | c | 10. | a |

## **E**xercises to Help You

### Using Modal Verbs: *can/can't, must, should*

Use examples such as these to clarify meaning.

*Can/can't* to express present ability or lack of ability:

> The doctor will do everything he *can* to help Joanna.
> Joanna *can't* believe that she will get better.

*Must* to express necessity in the present or the future:

> Joanna *must* want to live.
> Joanna *must* believe she will get well.

*Should* to express advisability:

> Joanna *should* think about getting well.
> Joanna *should* do what the doctor says.

Invite students to create other sentences using modals to talk about what Joanna and Sue *can, must,* and *should* do.

Assign Exercises A, B, and C on pages 81–83. If the exercises are done in class, students may work in pairs or groups to complete them.

### Exercise A

Students' sentences will vary. Suggested answers:

1. They lived in a small apartment.
2. Greenwich Village is in New York City.
3. They loved to paint.
4. Their apartment had beautiful, big windows.
5. Joanna stayed in bed all day.
6. She must believe she will get well.
7. Joanna wanted to go to Italy.
8. She wanted to paint the Bay of Naples.

### Exercise B

1. d  Many artists are poor.
2. c  Their apartment had beautiful, big windows.
3. a  Joanna got into bed because she felt sick.
4. b  She stayed in bed all day.
5. b  Joanna did not eat.
6. d  She thought she would not get better.
7. c  Sue was very worried about Joanna.
8. a  The doctor said that Joanna must want to live.

## Exercise C

| | |
|---|---|
| 1. rent | 5. breathe |
| 2. apartment | 6. day after day |
| 3. artists | 7. brick |
| 4. cough | 8. moment |

### Forming Past Tense Questions

Use pairs of questions and answers like these to check students' understanding of word order in past tense sentences and questions. First, write a question on the board and ask a volunteer to give the answer; then write an answer and ask a volunteer to form a question.

> Who *were* Sue and Joanna?
> Sue and Joanna *were* friends.

> Joanna *stared* at a red brick wall.
> What *did* Joanna *stare* at all day?

You might write out past tense questions on slips of paper and cut the words apart. Students can arrange the slips to change questions to answers and vice versa. Provide extra slips for past tense questions with *did.*

Assign Exercises D, E, and F on pages 83–85.

### Exercise D

1. What were Sue and Joanna?
2. What were Joanna and Sue?
3. What did Sue and Joanna love to do?
4. What did Joanna do all day?
5. What did Joanna often say?
6. What did Joanna want to paint?

### Exercise E
#### Part A

| | |
|---|---|
| 1. F | 4. F |
| 2. T | 5. F |
| 3. F | 6. T |

### Exercise E
#### Part B

The structure of students' sentences may vary.

a. Sue and Joanna lived in New York City.
b. Joanna got sick in November.
c. Joanna thought that she would die.
d. Joanna did not eat.

### Exercise F

Students' sentences will vary.

## haring with Others

Have students work with partners or in groups to complete the activity on page 85 orally. Remind them to use vocabulary from the *sickness* word map that they started in the Warm Up.

When students choose which of the topics they are going to write about, suggest they begin by using a graphic organizer such as the Main Idea chart, page T1.

Have students share their writing by displaying it on a table or on a bulletin board or by reading it aloud. ■

# The Last Leaf

**P a r t  T w o ,  p a g e s  8 6 - 9 3**

## Warm Up

Do any or all of the following activities.

### Sequencing and Summarizing

Compose a brief summary of the story thus far and write each sentence on a separate strip of paper. Give the strips to a pair or small group of students. Have them put the strips in order and then summarize the story without looking at the strips. Then have students predict what they think will happen next in the story.

### Brainstorming

Draw or show a painter's palette. Have students think of as many words for art tools, materials, and other related concepts as they can in two minutes. List their words on the board and add any additional key words.

## Read the Selection

Have students follow along in their books as you play track 24 on the Level Three CD or read aloud lines 1–14 on page 86. You may want to stop at this point to check comprehension. Ask any or all of the following questions.

1. What does Joanna see out the window?
2. Why are the leaves on the vine falling?
3. Why is Joanna counting the leaves on the vine?

Check understanding of the key vocabulary. Encourage students to read for general meaning and not to worry about every word in the selection.

Play CD track 25 or read lines 15–28 on page 86. Use any or all of the following questions to check students' understanding.

1. What did Sue want to know?
2. What did Joanna say to Sue about the leaves?
3. Why is Joanna waiting for the last leaf to fall?

At this point you may want students to give an oral summary of the text so far and predict what they think will happen next.

Play CD track 26 or read lines 29–40 on page 87. Use questions such as the following to check understanding.

1. What surprising belief does Joanna have?
2. How does Sue first react to Joanna's belief?
3. What do you think will happen next?

Play CD track 27 or read the rest of the selection, lines 41–52 on page 87. Check understanding using any or all of the following questions.

1. What does Sue ask Joanna to do?
2. Why does Sue want to draw in Joanna's room?
3. Joanna says she wants to "go sailing down, down, down, like one of those poor, tired leaves." What does she mean?

## Model a Strategy:
## Visualizing a Story

Say: "When I read, I try to picture in my mind what is happening. In this part of the story, I try to picture the red brick wall and the leaves. I try to imagine the cold wind blowing them off the vine, one by one. I try to imagine how sad Joanna feels as she watches the leaves."

As you continue reading the story with the class, ask individuals what they are picturing as they read.

### Understanding Time Relationships

Write the words *past*, *present*, and *future* on the board. Have students look for time words on pages 86–87. Help them put the words into each category and write them in the correct column on the board. Examples include the following: *past*— three days ago, once, then; *present*—now; *future*—soon. Have the students work in groups to put the events mentioned on these pages into chronological order.

## You Can Answer These Questions

You may want to have students do this activity as classwork or as homework.

1. b          6. c
2. c          7. c
3. c          8. b
4. c          9. a
5. a         10. c

## Exercises to Help You

### Using the Past Tense: Irregular Verbs

Ask and write questions about the story to elicit examples of irregular verbs in the past tense. For example: Where *did* Sue *go*? (She *went* into Joanna's room.) What *did* Sue *take* into Joanna's room? (She *took* some drawing paper.) Whom *did* Sue *speak* to? (She *spoke* to Joanna.) What *did* the wind *blow* down? (The wind *blew* down the leaves.)

Write the questions and responses on the board. Guide students to notice the irregular forms and then to ask and answer additional questions about the story and about themselves using these verbs.

Assign Exercises A, B, C, and D on pages 89–91. Students can work in pairs or groups to complete them as classwork or you can assign the exercises for homework.

*Exercise A*
Students' sentences will vary. Suggested answers:

1. Sue took some drawing paper.
2. Sue drew beautiful pictures.
3. Sue used the money she earned to help pay the rent.
4. Joanna was counting.
5. Sue saw a long vine.
6. Joanna was waiting for the last leaf to fall.
7. Sue wanted to give Joanna some hot soup.
8. Joanna wanted to see the last leaf fall.

*Exercise B*

1. c Sue saw Joanna lying on the bed.
2. d The vine was climbing up the brick wall.
3. a There were only a few leaves left on the vine.
4. b It will be winter soon.
5. c Joanna turned toward the window.
6. d Sue told Joanna to think about getting well.
7. b Joanna said that she was not hungry.
8. a She closed her eyes because she was tired.

*Exercise C*

1. desk      4. stronger
2. rent      5. leaf
3. draw      6. of course

*Exercise D*

1. took      4. spoke
2. drew      5. went
3. blew

## Using Prenominal Adjectives and Indefinite Articles

Write these sentences on the board. Check understanding by asking students to add *a*, *an*, or *some* plus one of these adjectives.

     good    green    hot    long

1. She saw _____ _____ vine.
2. There were _____ _____ leaves on the vine.
3. Sue was _____ _____ artist.
4. Sue wanted to bring Joanna _____ _____ soup.

Help students explain when to use each of the indefinite articles: *some* for plural nouns, *a* and *an* for singular nouns, *an* before a noun that begins with a vowel. You may want to point out that there is only one form for adjectives.

Assign Exercises E and F on pages 92–93.

*Exercise E*
***Part A***

1. beautiful      4. long
2. cold      5. hot
3. red

*Exercise E*
***Part B***
Students' sentences will vary.

*Exercise F*
Students' sentences will vary.

## Predicting Outcomes

Ask students how they think the story "The Last Leaf" will end. Will Joanna die, or will there be a happy ending? Encourage students to give reasons for their opinions. Pass around an envelope. Have each student put in a slip of paper with his or her name on it and a prediction about how the story will end. Seal the envelope and open it at the end of the story to see who predicted correctly.

## Sharing with Others

Have students work with partners or in groups to complete the activity on page 93 orally.

When students choose which of the topics they are going to write about, suggest they begin by using a graphic organizer such as the T-Chart on page xi. Students can consider reasons for and against their position and enter them on the chart. They can then choose the best reasons to support their idea.

Have students share their writing by displaying it on a table or bulletin board or by reading it aloud. ■

# The Last Leaf

Part Three, pages 94-101

## Warm Up

Use any or all of the activities below.

### Finding the Main Idea

You may want to ask students to suggest possible titles for Part Two of the story as a way to help them focus on the main idea of the selection. Arrange students in pairs or small groups to prepare titles. Have students share their ideas with the class. List the ideas on the board.

### Using a Graphic Organizer

Make a T-Chart on the board. Label the headings *Joanna* and *Sue*. Ask students to identify some of the things that Joanna has done so far in the story. List students' suggestions in the proper column. Then encourage students to recall what Sue's reactions were to Joanna's actions. Invite students to consider what their own personal reaction might be to Joanna.

### Using an Illustration

Draw or bring in a picture of an apartment building. Use the picture to introduce vocabulary associated with building features. List the words on the board. Be sure to include *building, door, wall, upstairs, downstairs.*

## Read the Selection

Ask students to follow along on page 94 of their books as you play CD track 28 or read aloud lines 1–13. Check students' understanding of the passage.

1. Who lives downstairs from Joanna and Sue?
2. Why does Sue go to see Mr. Behrman?
3. What jobs does Behrman have? How long has he been an artist?

Check understanding of the key vocabulary in the selection. Encourage students to make predictions about how the new character will feature in the story.

Play CD track 29 or read lines 14–40 on pages 94–95. Check comprehension of the passage by using any or all of the following questions.

1. How did Behrman feel when he heard about Joanna's belief?
2. What will Behrman do someday?
3. Why did Sue and Behrman have fear in their eyes (lines 36–37)?

Complete the reading or play CD track 30 for lines 41–59 on page 95. Use any or all of these questions to check students' understanding.

1. Why did Joanna want the window shade raised?
2. What did Joanna see outside the window? What did the leaf look like?
3. Do you think this last leaf will fall?

Stop and allow students to think about what happened in this selection. Encourage them to guess how the characters felt when they saw the leaf still there on the wall. Help students summarize and record the information and events on their Story Elements chart. Review key vocabulary.

Demonstrate filling in the names and character information in the appropriate sections of the diagram. Encourage students to add other similarities and differences between the two characters. Help the class summarize the information on the chart.

## Ⓨou Can Answer These Questions

This activity can be assigned as classwork or as homework.

| | | | |
|---|---|---|---|
| 1. | c | 6. | b |
| 2. | a | 7. | c |
| 3. | b | 8. | b |
| 4. | c | 9. | a |
| 5. | a | 10. | b |

## Ⓔxercises to Help You

### Using *There is/There are/ There was/There were*

Help students to talk about the present location of objects in the classroom using *There is/There are*. Ask questions to elicit statements. For example: How many windows are there in this room? Are there any books on the table? List some of the sentences on the board. Point out the use of *There is* for singular objects and *There are* for plurals. Use the sentences on the board to demonstrate using *There was/There were* to describe past location of objects.

Now:
*There is* one door.
*There are* nine chairs in the room.

Yesterday:
*There was* one door.
*There were* eight chairs yesterday.

Encourage students to use *There was/ There were* to talk about the story. Alternatively, have students look through pages 94–95 for examples of *There was/ There were*.

Students can do Exercises A, B, and C on pages 97–99. You may want to arrange students in pairs or groups to complete the exercises as classwork or assign them for homework.

*Exercise A*
Students' sentences will vary. Suggested answers:

1. Mr. Behrman lived in the building.
2. Behrman had been painting for more than forty years.
3. Nobody bought Behrman's paintings.
4. Behrman dreamed of painting a great picture.
5. Behrman earned money by driving a taxi.
6. She wanted to draw him.
7. The leaf was bright green.
8. She thought it would fall during the night.

*Exercise B*

1. d Sue was going to draw a picture of an old man with a beard.
2. a Mr. Behrman saw that Sue was very unhappy.
3. b He was sad because Joanna was sick.
4. c She asked him to sit in a chair by the window.
5. a Joanna asked Sue to raise the window shade.
6. d There still was one leaf against the brick wall.
7. b She thought the leaf would fall during the night.
8. c Sue told Joanna to think about getting better.

*Exercise C*

1. downstairs
2. vacation
3. art
4. ill
5. shade
6. howled

**Identifying Adverbs**

Write on the board:

Sue walked into the room. She was quiet.
Sue walked *quietly* into the room.

Guide students to compare the sentences. Point out the *-ly* on the adverb. Explain that *quietly* in this sentence describes how Sue walked. Write other sentences and invite volunteers to rewrite them using an adverb.

The leaf hung on the vine. The leaf was brave.
The artist painted a picture. He was sad.

Have students look back through pages 94–95 for other examples of adverbs ending in *-ly*. If students ask, explain that for adjectives that end in *-y*, we change the *-y* to *-i* before adding the ending *-ly*.

Assign Exercises D, E, and F on pages 99–101.

*Exercise D*
*Part A*

1. quietly
2. bravely
3. slowly
4. angrily

*Exercise D*
*Part B*
Students' sentences will vary.

*Exercise E*

1. Mr. Behrman lived in the building.
2. They saw the brick wall.
3. She was staring at the window.
4. The leaf had yellow edges.
5. I want you to sit by the window.

*Exercise F*
Students' sentences will vary.

## Sharing with Others

Read the questions on page 101 together and encourage students to make inferences about what the characters saw and how they felt. You may want to have students look back and reread parts of pages 94–95 to look for details on which to base their inferences. Arrange students in pairs or small groups for discussion.

After students choose which question to answer in writing, give them a copy of the Main Idea chart on page T1 for recording their ideas before writing. After they write their individual answers, encourage them to work with partners to read and help edit each others' work.

Display students' work on a bulletin board or table or have students share their writing aloud. Encourage listeners to comment on what they like about others' work. ∎

# The Last Leaf

Part Four, pages 102–109

## Warm Up

Use any or all of the activities below.

### Summarizing and Using an Illustration

Revisit the illustration on page 76 and ask students to use the pictures to help retell the important events of the story. Encourage students to use details to support the main points of the story. Then have students look back at the Story Elements chart to compare their retelling with the information they have written.

### Asking Reader-Generated Questions

As a group, prepare questions that students would like to have answered about the story and characters and the illustration on page 103. For example: Is Joanna going to get better? In the illustration, Behrman has some paints. Is he going to paint something? List the questions on the board and have students see if the questions are answered after they read the final section of the story.

## Read the Selection

Have students follow along on page 102 of their books as you play CD track 31 or read aloud lines 1–16. Ask questions to check understanding of the passage.

1. What did Joanna look at all day?
2. What was the weather like that night?

3. Why did Joanna say she was wrong?
4. How do you think Joanna will act now?

Check understanding of the key vocabulary and the information in the selection. Encourage students to guess how Joanna will change after realizing she was wrong.

Play CD track 32 or read lines 17–32 on pages 102–103. Use any or all of the following questions to check students' comprehension.

1. What does Joanna want?
2. What did the doctor say about Joanna?
3. Whom else was the doctor visiting in the building?
4. What do you think happened to Mr. Behrman?

Ask students to tell what changes have happened to Joanna and Mr. Behrman. Complete the story by reading lines 33–47 or playing CD track 33. Check understanding with questions.

1. What happened to Mr. Behrman? Why did he get sick?
2. Where did the police find his brushes and a ladder?
3. What was Behrman's greatest work?
4. What kind of a person do you think Mr. Behrman was?

Ask students if they were surprised by the ending. Open the sealed envelopes and check to see if any of the predictions that students made about the story were correct. Review key vocabulary.

## Model a Strategy:
## Using a Graphic Organizer for Comparing and Contrasting

Create a T-Chart on the board and orally model making comparisons and contrasts about the characters to show if or how they changed from the beginning of the story to the conclusion. Write key information on the chart. Encourage students to give their own observations about the characters.

| At the beginning | At the end |
|---|---|
| Joanna was sick. | Joanna was getting better. |
| Joanna did not want to live. | Joanna wanted to live and travel. |

Distribute copies of the T-Chart on page xi. Have students copy the information from the board and then continue filling in information about the other characters in the story.

## **Y**ou Can Answer These Questions

You can assign this activity as classwork or as homework.

1. c
2. a
3. b
4. b
5. a
6. b
7. c
8. a
9. b
10. a

## **E**xercises to Help You

### Using the Past Tense:
### Irregular Verbs

Write and ask questions about the story using the past tense.

Where *did* the last leaf *hang?*

When *did* Behrman *make* the picture on the wall?

Where *did* the police *find* the brushes?

Help students respond using the irregular past tense forms. Write the responses on the board and point out the spelling changes. Invite students to create their own questions about the story using these verbs.

Assign Exercises A, B, C, and D on pages 105–107. You may want to arrange students in pairs or groups to complete the exercises as classwork or assign them for homework.

### *Exercise A*

Students' sentences will vary. Suggested answers:

1. Joanna looked out the window all day.
2. Joanna asked for some soup and some tea.
3. Joanna wanted to paint the Bay of Naples.
4. The doctor was sending Mr. Behrman to the hospital.
5. Mr. Behrman was sick for two days.
6. The police found a ladder, brushes, and paint.
7. Mr. Behrman painted the leaf on the brick wall.
8. Mr. Behrman painted it the night the last leaf fell.

### *Exercise B*

1. c Although it was dark, she could still see the leaf.
2. d At night Sue pulled down the window shade.
3. a Joanna said that she wanted to sit up.
4. b The doctor told Sue that Joanna was getting better.
5. b Mr. Behrman had been out all night.
6. c He had been outside in the rain and the snow.
7. d The last leaf never moved.
8. a Mr. Behrman painted the leaf after the last leaf fell.

### Exercise C

1. turned off
2. comfortable
3. soaking
4. ladder
5. pillows
6. foolish

### Exercise D

1. hung
2. made
3. found
4. sat
5. fell

## Using Prepositions

Write the following prepositions on the board:

for   in   behind   out   to   against

Point out that these prepositions are used to talk about location of objects. Explain that *for* can be used to talk about length of time: We're going to read *for* five minutes.

Ask students to look back through the story on pages 102–103 for examples of these prepositions.

Assign Exercises E and F on pages 108–109.

### Exercise E

1. out
2. in
3. to
4. against
5. for
6. behind

### Exercise F

Students' sentences will vary.

## Sharing with Others

Read the questions on page 109 together. Talk about phrases used to express opinions. You might want to list some of them on the board for students to refer to during the pair and group discussion time.

I think that...

In my opinion...

Students should choose one of the questions and then use a copy of the T-Chart, page xi, to organize their ideas and supporting details before writing.

Arrange a time for students to share their writing with the rest of the class. After students read their opinions, encourage others to ask questions and comment on ideas that they liked. ■

# Answers for Unit 3: The Last Leaf

(The Unit Assessment appears on the following page.)

1. Joanna believed that she would die when the last leaf fell.
2. Behrman painted a leaf on the wall.
3. Joanna got better but Behrman got sick and died.
4. Joanna and Sue were artists in New York City.
5. Joanna became very sick.
6. Joanna and Sue were artists in New York City.
7. Joanna became very sick.
8. Joanna believed that she would die when the last leaf fell.
9. Behrman painted a leaf on the wall.
10. Joanna got better but Behrman got sick and died.

11. brick
12. improving
13. apartment
14. float
15. cough
16. some
17. an
18. a
19. took
20. went

21.-22. Student questions will vary. Suggested responses:

Who took a trip to Italy last year?

Where did they go in Italy?

Name _____ Date _____

# The Last Leaf

**A s s e s s m e n t**

**A.** Complete these sentences by drawing lines from the first part to the second part. Write the complete sentences on the lines below, in the same order they happened in the story.

1. Joanna believed that she would     artists in New York City.
2. Behrman painted     very sick.
3. Joanna got better     die when the last leaf fell.
4. Joanna and Sue were     a leaf on the wall.
5. Joanna became     but Behrman got sick and died.

6. _____
7. _____
8. _____
9. _____
10. _____

**B.** Complete each sentence by adding the correct word.

apartment     cough     brick     float     improving

11. The wall of the building is made of red _____.

12. Joanna was sick but she is _____ now.

13. Do you live in a house or in an _____?

14. The leaf is light. It can _____ in the wind.

15. What's the matter? I have a _____ and it is hard to breathe.

**C.** Fill in each blank using *a*, *an*, or *some*.

16. Please bring _____ more soup.

17. Behrman was _____ artist.

18. He painted _____ great picture on the wall.

**D.** Fill in each blank using the past tense of the verb in parentheses. Then change the sentences into questions. Write the questions on the lines below.

19. Joanna and Sue _____ a trip to Italy last year. (take)

20. They _____ to Naples to paint the bay. (go)

21. _____
22. _____

# The Hero
pages 111–135

# Planning Guide

## Part 1
pages 111–119

Using resources

Classifying

Asking reader-generated questions

Visualizing a story

Using the past tense: irregular verbs

Using prepositions of location

## Part 2
pages 120–127

Dramatizing

Drawing a picture

Summarizing

Identifying problems and solutions

Understanding multiple meanings

Using the future tense: *will*

Changing adjectives to adverbs

## Part 3
pages 128–135

Sequencing and summarizing

Drawing conclusions

Using two-word phrasal verbs

Changing statements to questions: *how*

# Vocabulary

| Story Words | Words Relating to the Military | Words Relating to Getting Water | Idioms |
|---|---|---|---|
| to cheer | to salute | to lower | to fool around |
| to crawl | | to spill | to shut up |
| to dare | captain | to splash | |
| to offer | enemy | | over and over |
| to rush | flame | bucket | |
| to slap | flash | chain | |
| | rifle | cord | |
| edge | smoke | thirst | |
| | soldier | | |
| crazy | terror | | |
| worse | uniform | | |
| | | | |
| | wounded | | |

# The Hero

**pages 111-135**

## Story Synopsis

*Note:* This story deals with a war situation, which may be a sensitive issue for some students depending on their past experiences.

Fred Collins, a soldier in the army during the American Civil War, had been fighting with his troop all day. He was thirsty. He saw a well near an old house, but to get there, someone would have to cross a battlefield full of flying bullets. Other soldiers laughed at the idea and dared Collins to go. Collins, to prove his bravery, asked the captain for permission to attempt to reach the well. After a wild run across the field, Collins filled a water bottle. Then terror seized him. He filled the well bucket with water and began running back with it. Collins paused to give some water to a wounded man on the field. He then continued his panicked run back to his group with the bucket of water. The captain said to let the men drink first. The first two men to receive the bucket began laughing and pushing and pulling each other. The bucket fell to the ground, and no one had any water.

## About the Author

Stephen Crane was born in Newark, New Jersey, in 1871. He became a newspaper reporter and worked as a war correspondent in Mexico, Cuba, and Greece. His stories are often about people being alone and the fear of being alone. His most famous book, *The Red Badge of Courage*, takes place during the Civil War. Crane's characters seem real, with both strong points and natural weaknesses. Stephen Crane died in 1900.

Bring in a picture of Stephen Crane or have students look through a reference book for a picture and biography of the author. Guide discussion of any pictures students find. What did Stephen Crane look like? Was he old or young? What kind of clothes was he wearing? What kind of a person do you think he was?

Have students locate on a map Crane's birthplace (Newark, New Jersey) and the countries where he worked as a war correspondent.

Stephen Crane was a newspaper reporter. Invite students to pretend they are reporters and prepare questions they would like to ask Stephen Crane in an interview. Students can then ask you their questions. If possible, give the answers or bring in resource books and help students find the answers. Have students work in pairs or small groups to write up their "interviews."

# Introducing the Story

Have students look at the opening illustration on page 110. Guide discussion of the characters and setting pictured. Encourage students to point out and comment on details in the picture. Use the questions on page 111 to help focus the discussion.

*Note:* Accept a variety of responses during the discussion. Encourage students to point out details in the illustrations that support their ideas. Explain that there is no one "right" answer to these questions. Remind students that they will find out if their predictions are accurate as they read through the story.

## Vocabulary Option

Ask students to name objects, feelings, and actions that they see in the picture. As students identify items, list the words on the board or on chart paper. Add new words to the list as students read through the story.

## Writing Option

You may want students to write out a simple story or character study based only on the picture. Students can work individually or in pairs. Encourage students to use words from the vocabulary list. Post the stories and descriptions on the classroom wall and compare and contrast students' writings with the actual story.

# The Hero

Part One, pages 111–119

## Warm Up

Do any or all of the following activities.

### Using Resources

Bring in encyclopedias and other resource materials on the Civil War. Explain that the story takes place during this time. Invite students to use the resource materials to find information about the war. Students can work in pairs or small groups to fill in the information they find on a chart such as this one. As a group, review what students learned and recorded on their charts.

When _____

Where _____

Who _____

Uniform Colors _____

Flags _____

### Classifying

Write column headings on the board:

*Sights   Sounds   Smells   Feelings*

Then ask students to look over the words that they listed about soldiers and armies in the Vocabulary Option and decide if these would be things that they see, hear, smell, or feel. After students have written the words in the appropriate columns, encourage them to think of other things in a war situation that relate to the senses.

## Asking Reader-Generated Questions

Before reading the story, have students consider the illustration and title and prepare questions they would like answered about the story. Record students' questions on chart paper and use the questions to help set purposes for reading.

After each part of the story, check to see if any of the reader-generated questions have been answered.

## Read the Selection

Have students follow along on page 112 of their books as you play track 34 on the CD or read lines 1–24 aloud. You may want to stop at this point to check for understanding. Ask any or all of the following questions. Students may answer individually or in groups.

1.  Why were the men tired and thirsty?
2.  What did Fred Collins wish he had?
3.  Who was on the horse? Why did the horse and rider fall?
4.  Where was the well? What did Collins think was in the well?

Check understanding of key vocabulary. Help students realize that it is not necessary to know the meaning of every word to get the general meaning of a passage. Point out the author's use of sensory description to give the reader a feeling of being there.

Play track 35 on the CD or read lines 25–46 on page 113. Check for understanding using any or all of the following questions.

1. What was happening on the field?
2. What happened to the house when a shell struck it?
3. Who was laughing at Collins? Why were they laughing?
4. What did Collins say he would do? Why did he say that?

Help students make an oral summary of the story so far including a description of the setting, main character, and problem. As they summarize, write the key ideas on the board and review key vocabulary.

### Model a Strategy:
### Visualizing a Story

Say: "When I'm reading a story, the author sometimes clearly describes people and places. I can see, hear, and smell what is happening."

Have students close their eyes as you reread lines 1–2. Ask students to describe the picture they get in their minds from the information in the story. Encourage students to look through pages 112–113 for other descriptive portions of the story.

Give students a copy of the Story Elements chart, page xii, and have them work in pairs or small groups to fill in information on the setting, characters, and problem.

## You Can Answer These Questions

Students can do the comprehension activity in class or as homework.

| | | | |
|---|---|---|---|
| 1. | c | 6. | b |
| 2. | c | 7. | b |
| 3. | b | 8. | a |
| 4. | c | 9. | c |
| 5. | a | 10. | a |

## Exercises to Help You

### Using the Past Tense: Irregular Verbs

Write these past tense verb forms on the board:

threw    flew    had    struck    shook

Ask students to look back through the story on pages 112–113 for examples of the verbs. As students point out examples, write them on the board.

Use the examples to help elicit past tense questions using *did* and the base forms of the verbs.

> Bullets *flew*. *Did* bullets *fly*?
>
> The soldier *threw* up his hands. *Did* the soldier *throw* up his hands?
>
> I *had* a drink. *Did* you *have* a drink?
>
> A shell *struck* the old house. *Did* a shell *strike* the old house?
>
> Collins *shook* his fist. *Did* Collins *shake* his fist?

Invite volunteers to create other questions about the story, characters, and setting using these verbs.

Have students work on Exercises A, B, C, and D on pages 115–117. If the exercises are done in class, students may complete the work in pairs or groups.

*Exercise A*

Students' sentences will vary. Suggested answers:

1. The army had been fighting all day.
2. The men felt tired.
3. Fred Collins wanted a drink of water.
4. The soldier fell to the ground.
5. The well was near the barn.
6. Collins got angry because he saw the soldiers laughing.
7. He went to find the captain.

*Exercise B*

1. b   They saw a horse with a soldier on its back.
2. d   The soldier tried to cover his face.
3. a   The old house was falling down.
4. c   Fred Collins shook his head and turned away.
5. c   Collins thought there was water in the well.
6. a   Pieces of earth were thrown in the air.
7. d   All the soldiers laughed at Collins.
8. b   Collins said he wasn't afraid to go.

*Exercise C*

1. smoke          4. worse
2. soldiers       5. dared
3. rushed         6. captain

*Exercise D*

1. threw          4. struck
2. flew           5. shook
3. had

## Using Prepositions of Location

Write these prepositions on the board:

around    at    by    across

Model sentences about people and objects in the room and use gestures to clarify the meanings of the prepositions of location. For example: My book is *around* here (as you motion with your hand the area where your book can be found). We are *at* school (use a motion to indicate a specific place). Carlos sits *by* the window (motion to show near or on the side). I will walk *across* the room (walk from one side to the other).

Have students use the prepositions to describe the location of other people and objects in the room.

Assign Exercises E and F on pages 118–119.

*Exercise E*

1. with           4. across
2. around         5. of
3. at             6. by

*Exercise F*

Students' sentences will vary.

## Sharing with Others

Have students work with partners or in small groups to complete the activity on page 119 orally. Remind students to use vocabulary from the word list created in the Vocabulary Option.

Have students choose one question to answer in writing. You may want to have them use a graphic organizer such as the Main Idea chart, page T1, to record their ideas before they begin writing. If they choose the second option, they may want to write a dialogue instead of a paragraph.

Have students share their writing by displaying it or by reading it aloud. ∎

# The Hero

Part Two, pages 120–127

## Warm Up

Do any or all of the following activities.

### Dramatizing

Have students dramatize portions of Part One. They can use the various dialogues on pages 112–113 or improvise their own. You may want to have some students work on sound effects to add to the dramatization.

### Drawing a Picture

Give students the opportunity to create a drawing or picture based on the descriptive passages of Part One. If students do not want to draw, they can make a collage using magazine or newspaper pictures. Encourage students to share and explain their pictures to the class.

### Summarizing

Have students use the information that they have written on their Story Elements chart as notes to help retell the first part of the story and explain the problem. Invite a volunteer to state the events in order and have others add other information as needed.

## Read the Selection

Have students follow along in their books as you play CD track 36 or read aloud lines 1–20 on page 120. Stop and check students' understanding of the passage. Ask any or all of the following questions.

1. How did Collins greet the captain?
2. What did Collins want to do?
3. Did the captain say yes or no? Did the captain want Collins to go or did he want Collins to wait? Why do you think so?

Check understanding of the vocabulary. Encourage students to read for general meaning and not to worry about every word in the selection.

Play track 37 on the CD or read lines 21–40 on pages 120–121. Use any or all of the following questions to check students' understanding.

1. What did the other soldiers do before Collins left?
2. How did Collins feel at this point?
3. Were the other soldiers surprised that Collins was going? How do you know?
4. Do you think Collins went because he was really so thirsty, or was it because somebody dared him?

At this point you may have students give an oral summary of the text so far. Encourage them to comment on dares and challenges and how they can motivate people to do things that might be risky.

Play CD track 38 or read lines 41–60 on page 121. Use questions such as the following to check understanding.

1. Why did Collins stop at the edge of the field? How did he feel?
2. How far did Collins walk before the enemy fired their rifles?
3. What did Collins see in the well?
4. How did Collins feel after he got to the well?

## Model a Strategy: Using a Graphic Organizer: Identifying Problems and Solutions

Draw a T-Chart on the board and label the column headings: *Problem, Solution.* Say: "As I read, I try to remember important events. In Part One, there was a problem: Collins was thirsty and wanted to get to the well. Now in this part, he got to the well. That's the solution to the first problem."

Write the problem and solution on the chart. Help students identify the new problem that occurred at the bottom of page 121 and write it on their charts. As you continue reading the story with the class, remind students to look for the next problem and its solution.

## Understanding Multiple Meanings

Write the word *face* on the board. Invite volunteers to explain or show what the word means. Explain that *face* has several meanings including the front side of the head and the action of turning so you can be across from an object or person. Now ask students to look at line 44: He had to face death. Encourage students to consider how the word *face* is used in this sentence and what the sentence means.

## You Can Answer These Questions

You may want to have students do this activity as classwork or as homework.

| | | | |
|---|---|---|---|
| 1. | b | 6. | a |
| 2. | c | 7. | c |
| 3. | b | 8. | a |
| 4. | c | 9. | b |
| 5. | a | 10. | c |

## Exercises to Help You

### Using the Future Tense: *will*

Make a T-Chart on the board. Add headings: *Now, Future.* Ask students questions about where Collins is now (at this point in the story) and predict what he will do next. Write in students' responses in the appropriate columns. See example below.

Call attention to the verb forms used in the future tense. Point out the use of *will* with the base form of the verb. Invite students to talk about their own future plans using *will.*

Assign Exercises A, B, C, and D on pages 123–125. Students can work in pairs or groups to complete the exercises as classwork or you can assign them for homework.

### Exercise A

Students' sentences will vary. Suggested answers:

1. Collins wanted to get some water.
2. The captain told Collins to bring back some water.
3. Collins said he would get the water.
4. He saw water at the bottom of the well.
5. Collins took the cap off the water bottle.
6. He dropped the bottle into the well.
7. Collins asked himself, "What am I doing here?"
8. He thought he was going to die.

| Now | Future |
|---|---|
| Collins *is* by the well. | Collins *will go* back. |
| He *is* getting water. | He *will take* water to the soldiers. |
| He *is* sitting on the ground. | He *will run* fast. |
| He *is* afraid. | He *will* … |

## Exercise B

1. b  Collins said there was water in the well.
2. c  The captain asked Collins to think about the danger.
3. d  For a moment, Collins thought he was in a dream.
4. a  He pulled down his cap and walked quickly away.
5. d  Collins walked thirty feet into the field.
6. c  He knew that the men were watching him.
7. b  He ran wildly toward the well and threw himself down on the ground.
8. a  Then suddenly he felt very weak.

## Exercise C

1. saluted
2. slapped
3. edge
4. crazy
5. enemy
6. thirst

## Exercise D
### Part A

1. will go
2. will get
3. will bring
4. will drink
5. will feel

## Exercise D
### Part B

Students' sentences will vary. Be sure that students write the future tense by using *will* plus the verb.

### Changing Adjectives to Adverbs

Write on the board:

Sue walked into the room. (quiet)
Sue walked *quietly* into the room.

Guide students to compare the sentences. Point out the *-ly* on the adverb. Explain that *quietly* in this sentence describes how Sue walked. Write other sentences and adjectives and invite volunteers to rewrite the sentences using an adverb.

Collins ran toward the well. (quick)
The men watched Collins. (careful)

Ask students to look back through pages 120–121 for other examples of adverbs ending in *-ly*.

Assign Exercises E and F on pages 126–127.

### Exercise E
### Part A

1. loudly
2. softly
3. bravely
4. quietly
5. sadly

### Exercise E
### Part B
Students' sentences will vary. Be sure that students add the suffix *-ly* to each adjective.

### Exercise F
Students' sentences will vary.

## 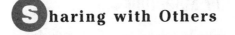haring with Others

Before assigning the activity on page 127, have students imagine that they are one of the characters in the story. Encourage them to discuss what their personal reactions would be. Then have students work with partners or in small groups to complete the activity on page 127 orally.

After students choose one of the topics to write about, suggest they use a graphic organizer such as the T-Chart on page xi. Students can consider and record possible reactions and give reasons to support the reactions on their charts. They can then choose the best reasons to support their idea.

Have students share their writing by making a writing display on a table or bulletin board or by inviting students to read their work aloud. ■

# The Hero

**Part Three, pages 128–135**

## Warm Up

Use any or all of the activities below.

### Sequencing and Summarizing

Prepare a brief summary of the story. Write each sentence of the summary on a strip of paper. Invite volunteers to arrange the strips in the correct order. Have one student read the strips while the others in the class listen and discuss if the order is correct or not.

## Read the Selection

Ask students to follow along on page 128 of their books as you play track 39 on the CD or read aloud lines 1–14. Check students' understanding of the passage.

1. How did Collins get water from the well?
2. Why did he run as fast as he could? How did he feel?
3. Do you think Collins will help the wounded soldier? Why or why not?

Check that students understand the key vocabulary in the selection. Encourage students to give their own personal reactions to the wounded man's request.

Play CD track 40 or read lines 15–30 on pages 128–129. Check comprehension of the passage by using any or all of the following questions.

1. Why didn't Collins stop at first for the wounded man?
2. Why do you think Collins went back to give the man a drink?
3. What did the other soldiers do when Collins got back?

Discuss if students' predictions about Collins's return were correct or not. Is Collins a hero? Why or why not? Point out that the story is not over and ask students if they can think of what else the author is going to tell us.

Complete the reading for lines 31–41 on page 129 or play CD track 41. Use any or all of these questions to check students' understanding.

1. Whom did Collins offer the bucket of water to?
2. Why did the captain not drink any water?
3. What happened to the bucket?
4. Did anyone drink the water? How do you think the soldiers felt? How did Collins feel?

Allow students time to think about what happened in this selection. Encourage them to guess how the characters felt at the end and to consider if Collins was a hero. Help students summarize and record the information and events on their Story Elements chart. Review key vocabulary.

## Model a Strategy:
## Drawing Conclusions

Say: "The author is telling a story for a reason. I wonder what the reason is. I need to stop and think about what has happened. Collins was a hero. He ran across a battlefield. He could have been killed. He got water and brought it back. But then the bucket of water fell and no one had any water. What does this tell me?"

Help students draw conclusions about the other soldiers' attitude toward Collins or their lack of appreciation for what he went through to get the water. Students can express their ideas on what the author is trying to say about human nature through this story.

## You Can Answer These Questions

This activity can be assigned as classwork or as homework.

1. b
2. c
3. c
4. a
5. c
6. a
7. b
8. c
9. a
10. a

## Exercises to Help You

### Using Two-word Phrasal Verbs

Use pairs of sentences to explain the difference in meaning between two-word phrasal verbs and the original verbs. Then act out the sentences and have students respond with the correct sentence that describes the actions.

Pull the box.
*Pull up* the box.

Run to the store.
*Run back* to the store.

Look at the tree.
*Look down* at the tree.

Ask a question.
*Ask for* a book.

Students can do Exercises A, B, and C on pages 131–133. You may want to arrange students in pairs or groups to complete them as classwork or assign the exercises for homework.

### Exercise A
Students' sentences will vary. Suggested answers:

1. He saw a wooden bucket on the ground.
2. When the bucket was full, he pulled it up.
3. He was afraid that he would be shot dead.
4. The man asked for a drink of water.
5. He could not lift his arm to take the water.
6. They cheered.
7. Two young soldiers were the first to get the bucket.
8. The bucket crashed to the ground.

### Exercise B

1. b  Collins looked down into the well.
2. c  When the bucket was full, he pulled it up.
3. d  Collins's cap fell off, and his hair flew wildly.
4. a  He turned and ran back to the wounded man.
5. b  The man could not lift his arm to take the water.
6. d  A few minutes later Collins was back with the men.
7. a  When one solder tried to drink, the other soldier pulled his arm.
8. c  The two soldiers stared at each other.

### Exercise C

1. flash
2. chain
3. splashed
4. cheered
5. offered
6. spill

### Changing Statements to Questions: *how*

Review how to change past tense statements into questions.

Write these question words on the board:

how     how much     how (long, fast, ...)

Write several past tense sentences and invite volunteers to create a question using *how* or one of the forms of *how*. Write the questions on the board. Point out the word order and verb forms in the sentences and corresponding questions. Some examples might be:

Collins *ran* quickly.
There *were* two soldiers.

*How did* Collins *run*?
*How many* soldiers *were* there?

Assign Exercises D, E, and F on pages 133–135.

*Exercise D*

1. How much water was in the bottle? or How full was the bottle?
2. How did Collins begin to feel?
3. How did Collins grab the bucket?
4. How fast did he run?
5. How happy were the two young soldiers?

*Exercise E*

1. Collins began to feel stronger.
2. He was afraid to stop running.
3. The man could not lift his arm.
4. Collins pulled the bucket away.
5. The bucket was lying on the ground.

*Exercise F*

Students' sentences will vary.

### Sharing with Others

Read the questions on page 135 together and encourage students to give their personal reactions to Collins's actions and the story's ending. Remind students that there is no one correct response to these types of questions.

After students have decided on which question to answer, you may want to give them a copy of the Main Idea chart on page T1 for recording their ideas before writing.

After students write their individual answers, encourage them to work with partners, reading and helping edit each others' work. Display students' work or have students share their writing aloud. Encourage listeners to comment on what they like about others' work. ■

# Answers for Unit 4: The Hero

1. A wounded soldier asked for water to drink.
2. Collins ran quickly across the field.
3. Two soldiers dropped the bucket.
4. A soldier dared Collins to get water.
5. He pulled up a bucket of water.

6. A soldier dared Collins to get water.
7. Collins ran quickly across the field.
8. He pulled up a bucket of water.
9. A wounded soldier asked for water to drink.
10. Two soldiers dropped the bucket.

11. smoke
12. cheered
13. dared
14. soldier
15. wounded

16. threw
17. had
18. flew
19. shook

20. slowly
21. quickly
22. sadly

23. How did he drink the cold water?
24. How did the horse jump over the fence?
25. How did we watch as they marched away?

**Name** _____ **Date** _____

# The Hero

**Assessment**

**A.** Complete these sentences by drawing lines from the first part to the second part. Write the complete sentences on the lines below, in the same order they happened in the story.

1. A wounded soldier      Collins to get water.
2. Collins ran quickly      dropped the bucket.
3. Two soldiers      across the field.
4. A soldier dared      a bucket of water.
5. He pulled up      asked for water to drink.

6. _____

7. _____

8. _____

9. _____

10. _____

**B.** Complete each sentence by adding the correct word.

**cheered**      **wounded**      **smoke**      **soldier**      **dared**

11. There was a lot of _____ with the fire.

12. All the soldiers _____ when Collins came back with the water.

13. "I don't think you can do it!" he _____ the man.

14. A _____ was holding a rifle.

15. The man fell from the horse. He was _____.

**C.** Fill in each blank using the past tense of the verb in parentheses.

16. The captain _____ a water bottle to the soldier. (throw)

17. I _____ a dream last night. (have)

18. The bird _____ through the air to the tree. (fly)

19. They _____ the man to wake him up. (shake)

**D.** Fill in each blank by changing the adjective in parentheses to an adverb. Then change the sentences into *how* questions.

20. He drank the cold water _____. (slow)

21. The horse jumped _____ over the fence. (quick)

22. We watched _____ as they marched away. (sad)

23. How _____

24. How _____

25. How _____

# Land
pages 137–166

# Planning Guide

## Part 1
pages 137–146

Using prior knowledge

Previewing the selection

Finding the main idea and supporting details

Using the past tense: regular and irregular verbs

Using object pronouns

## Part 2
pages 147–155

Using an illustration

Stopping and thinking

Using characterization to gain meaning

Using modals: *can/could*

Using possessive pronouns

## Part 3
pages 156–166

Understanding meaning associations

Understanding irony

Identifying verb tenses: past, present, future

Changing statements to questions

# Vocabulary

| Story Words | Words Relating to Buying and Selling | Words Relating to Clothing | Idioms |
|---|---|---|---|
| to flow | to agree | boots | to keep in mind |
| to lean | to own | fur | to take care of |
| to march | to rent | pocket | |
| to rise | | | at once |
| to wave | acre | | right now |
| to whisper | price | | |
| | ruble | | |
| cart | | | |
| direction | cheap | | |
| gift | greedy | | |
| grave | | | |
| oats | | | |
| pile | | | |
| shovel | | | |
| | | | |
| delighted | | | |
| possible | | | |
| seventh | | | |
| stupid | | | |

# Land

## Story Synopsis

Pakhom, a poor farmer, listened eagerly to a traveler who told of cheap farmland in the south of Russia. Pakhom decided to visit the Land of the Bashkirs and try to buy a large piece of land. Pakhom took his savings, bought some gifts, and left for the land of the Bashkirs. The chief of the Bashkirs offered land at 500 rubles a day—all the land you could walk around in one day for 500 rubles. The trick was to be sure to arrive back at the starting point before the sun set or you would lose all your money. Pakhom placed his money in the chief's hat and started walking. He dug holes along his route to mark his land. He kept seeing nice pieces of land and walking further. Finally realizing that he was far away, he hurried back to the starting point. At the bottom of the hill, it looked as if all was lost, but the sun was still shining on the hilltop. Pakhom struggled to get to the chief's hat and reached it just in time. Unfortunately, the greedy Pakhom died from the exertion.

## About the Author

Leo Tolstoy was one of Russia's most famous writers. He was born in Nikolaievsk (south of Moscow) in 1828. He wrote historic epics about Russian life in a very realistic style, with characters that seem very alive. Two of his most well-known novels are *War and Peace* and *Anna Karenina*. Tolstoy was a thinker who looked for the meaning of life. He dressed as a peasant and worked in the fields. Tolstoy died in 1910.

Have students look for pictures of Tolstoy in reference books. Ask students to describe Tolstoy in the pictures. How did he dress? What did he look like? Was he old or young in the picture? What was he doing in the picture?

Bring in a map of Europe or the world and have students find Russia, Moscow, and, if possible, Nikolaievsk (near Tula). Encourage students to share any information they know about the country and people of Russia.

You may want to bring in copies of some of Tolstoy's novels and have students comment on the length of the books. If there are pictures on the cover or illustrations in the books, have students discuss the people and scenes.

# Introducing the Story

Have students look at the opening illustration on page 136. Guide discussion of the characters and setting pictured. Encourage students to point out and comment on details in the picture. Use the questions on page 137 to help focus the discussion.

*Note:* As students share their ideas about the illustration, remind them that there are no "right" answers. Explain that illustrations can often be used to help clarify information and give clues about the plot and characters. Encourage students to support their answers with details from the picture, and accept any answer that can be logically supported. Students can find out if their predictions are accurate as they work through the story.

## Vocabulary Option

Use the illustration to review and introduce key vocabulary that will be in the story. Invite volunteers to identify and describe various places and objects in the picture. List the words on the board or on chart paper. Add new words to the list as students read through the story.

## Writing Option

Arrange students in small groups to prepare a character study based only on the picture. Students can use the "Introducing the Story" questions as a starting point. Encourage them to make inferences based on the pictures. Post the character studies on the classroom wall for future reference and comparison as students read the story.

## Cultural Observations Option

Ask students to look at the picture and talk about the cultural groups pictured. Do all these characters come from the same area of Russia? Based on the housing, land, and clothes in the illustration, what was life like for these people? How would their life be similar to ours? How would it be different?

# Land

## Warm Up

Do any or all of the following activities.

### Using Prior Knowledge

Make a T-Chart on the board. Have students explain how they buy things such as food, clothing, cars, or homes. Record types of purchases in the first column of the T-Chart and how the items are measured, priced, or bought in the second column (for example: *rice: pound; milk: gallon; clothing: sizes; land: acre*). Encourage students to talk about purchases they have made: how they found the store or item and who sold it to them.

### Previewing the Selection

Explain the setting of the story and introduce the name of the main character. Help students with the pronunciation of Bashkir (bahsh-KEER) and Pakhom (pah-KHOME). Ask students what kind of money is used in Russia (rubles). Allow students to talk about other currencies that they know from their native countries or places where they have traveled.

## Read the Selection

Have students follow along in their books on page 138 as you play track 42 of the Level Three CD or read lines 1–15 aloud. After reading, pause to check comprehension using any or all of the following questions.

1. What did Pakhom dream of? How large was his farm?
2. Did Pakhom work hard? How do you know?
3. Who stopped at Pakhom's house? Where was the traveler returning from?
4. How many acres of land did the traveler buy there? How many rubles did he pay for the land?

Check understanding of key vocabulary. Help students give descriptions of the two characters based on what they have read in the passage.

Play CD track 43 or read lines 16–43 on pages 138–139. Check for understanding, using any or all of the following questions.

1. What did the traveler think of the Bashkirs?
2. How could Pakhom make friends with the Bashkirs?
3. Was the land good or bad for farming? What was near the land?
4. Who was going to take care of the farm while Pakhom was gone?

Invite students to consider if they would go to the Land of the Bashkirs to buy land as Pakhom is planning. The traveler makes it seem like a good idea, but what questions might they have about the land?

Continue reading lines 44–69 on pages 139–140 or play CD track 44. Check students' understanding by asking questions.

1. When did Pakhom start on the trip? Who was going with him?
2. What did Pakhom bring in the cart?
3. What did the Bashkirs do when they saw Pakhom?
4. Did the Bashkirs agree to sell Pakhom some land? Whom were they waiting for?

At this point, help students make an oral summary of the story so far. As they summarize, write the key ideas on the board and review key vocabulary.

## Model a Strategy:
## Finding the Main Idea and
## Supporting Details

Model finding the main idea and supporting details of the selection. Say: "I will understand and remember the story better if I think about what the main idea of this first part of the story is. I think the main idea is that Pakhom wants to go to the Land of the Bashkirs and buy some of their land. What details can I remember that support this idea? One is that Pakhom has very little land himself. Another is that the Bashkirs will sell their land very cheaply."

Distribute copies of the Main Idea chart on page T1. Help students record the main idea and details that you modeled. Then have them work in pairs to find more details they can use to support the main idea.

# **Y**ou Can Answer
# These Questions

Students can do the comprehension activity in class or as homework.

| | | | |
|---|---|---|---|
| 1. | b | 6. | c |
| 2. | c | 7. | a |
| 3. | a | 8. | b |
| 4. | a | 9. | c |
| 5. | b | 10. | b |

# **E**xercises to Help You

## Using the Past Tense:
## Regular and Irregular Verbs

Make a T-Chart on the board. Label the columns *Regular Verbs* and *Irregular Verbs*. Ask questions in the past tense and invite volunteers to respond orally. The class can decide if the verb is regular or irregular in the past tense. Volunteers can write the base and past tense forms of the verbs in the proper column on the T-Chart. Some questions to use might be:

> Where did Pakhom live?
> What did he dream of?
> How long did Pakhom travel?
> What did the Bashkirs sell to the traveler?
> Where did the Bashkirs lead Pakhom?
> How much land did the traveler buy?

Students can work in pairs asking and answering questions about the story, using verbs in the past tense.

Assign Exercises A, B, C, and D on pages 142–144. You may want to have students work in pairs or groups to complete these exercises in class.

*Exercise A*
Students' sentences will vary.

1. Pakhom was a poor farmer.
2. He dreamed of having much land.
3. The traveler needed food for his horse.
4. Pakhom and the traveler drank tea.
5. It is in the south of Russia.
6. They owned many acres.
7. Pakhom bought some presents and two boxes of tea.
8. He gave them presents.
9. Pakhom wanted to buy a piece of land.
10. The Bashkirs were waiting for their Chief.

*Exercise B*

1. b  One day a traveler stopped at Pakhom's farm.
2. d  The traveler was coming back from the Land of the Bashkirs.
3. a  The traveler bought a large piece of land.
4. c  He said that the land cost almost nothing.
5. e  Pakhom told his wife about the Bashkirs.
6. c  Pakhom and his helper went to find the Bashkirs.
7. d  The helper pulled a heavy wooden cart.
8. b  The Bashkirs seemed to be happy people.
9. e  The Bashkirs gave Pakhom some food to eat.
10. a  The Bashkirs were waiting for their Chief.

*Exercise C*

1. oats
2. stupid
3. rubles
4. gifts
5. seventh
6. own

*Exercise D*

1. dreamed
2. stopped
3. lived
4. offered
5. talked
6. drank
7. bought
8. sold
9. led
10. gave

**Using Object Pronouns**

Write pairs of sentences on the board to illustrate use of object pronouns. For example:

I gave the tea to the traveler.
I gave *him* the tea.

I gave gifts to the Bashkirs.
I gave *them* gifts.

The worker pulled the wagon.
The worker pulled *it*.

Guide students to notice the differences between the two sentences. If needed, point out the words that are missing in the second sentence and the object pronoun that replaces the words. Write examples using the first and second person object pronouns and have students tell who is receiving the action.

Sonia gave *me* a book.

I told *you* the answer to the question.

Please send *us* a letter.

Assign Exercises E and F on pages 145–146.

*Exercise E*

1. them
2. it
3. you
4. me
5. him
6. you
7. us
8. her

*Exercise F*
Students' sentences will vary.

# Sharing with Others

Read the questions on page 146 together and guide students to make predictions about the story. Encourage students to look back through the story for details to help support their ideas. You may want to create a T-Chart on the board or on chart paper to record students' ideas and supporting details.

Students can choose their own topic for writing and copy the appropriate chart for their topic. Encourage students to circle or highlight the ideas that they want to include to support their predictions about the story.

Have students share their writing by displaying it on a table or bulletin board or by reading it aloud. ■

# Land

P a r t   T w o ,   p a g e s   1 4 7 – 1 5 5

## Warm Up

Do any or all of the following activities.

### Using an Illustration: Brainstorming

Have students look at the illustration of the Chief on page 148 and describe him. Students can think of words and phrases to describe his clothing, his facial expression, and his role as a leader or chief of his people. Make a list of students' suggestions on the board. Ask them if they would like to buy something from the Chief, and encourage them to explain their responses.

### Language Across the Curriculum
*Math: Perimeter and Area*

Draw a rectangle and square on the board. Label the sides of the rectangle *5 miles, 7 miles, 5 miles, 7 miles*. Ask students how far it would be to walk around this piece of land. Label the sides of the square *6 miles*. Students can compare the distance around the two shapes (perimeter) and the sizes (area) of the shapes. If these shapes were pieces of land, which one would students want to have? What other shape(s) would be possible with a perimeter of 24 miles?

## Read the Selection

Have students follow along in their books as you play CD track 45 or read aloud lines 1–34 on pages 147–148. You may want to stop at this point to check comprehension. Ask any or all of the following questions.

1. Who was wearing a large fur hat and coat? What did Pakhom give him?
2. What is the price of the land?
3. Does Pakhom think he will get a lot of land or a little? Why?
4. Where will Pakhom start? Where will he end?
5. What will happen if he takes too long?

Check understanding of the key vocabulary. Encourage students to read for general meaning and not to worry about every word in the selection. Students can check and revise previous predictions they have made based on what they have read.

Play CD track 46 or read lines 35–51 on page 148. Use any or all of the following questions to check students' understanding.

1. Why didn't Pakhom sleep that night?
2. What was Pakhom planning to do with the land?
3. Whom did Pakhom see in his dream? Why do you think the Chief was laughing in the dream?

At this point you may want students to consider what the dream may mean. Does it mean something good or bad will happen? Have students explain their interpretations.

Play CD track 47 or read lines 52–77 on pages 148–149. Use questions such as the following to check understanding.

1. What did Pakhom do when he woke up?
2. Why did the Chief put his hat on the ground? What did Pakhom put on the hat?
3. How did Pakhom get ready to start? Do you think he will get a lot of land? Why or why not?

## Model a Strategy: Stopping and Thinking

Say: "Sometimes I need to stop and ask myself if I understand what is happening. When I read about the dream, I was confused. The Chief was laughing. Was he laughing because he was happy or was he laughing at Pakhom? I'll look back and reread that section and see if I can find the answer."

Invite students to reread lines 41–51 and discuss what they think about Pakhom's dream. Guide students to notice how loudly the Chief/traveler is laughing.

## Using Characterization to Gain Meaning

Ask students to look at what they have written on the Story Elements chart about Pakhom. What additional words or phrases can they add to describe Pakhom? As a group, consider what Pakhom is constantly thinking about: land, lots of land, getting more land. Ask why Pakhom doesn't think about his farm, his wife, what he has. Ask whether students think it's good for a person to be so concerned with just one thing, as Pakhom is. Have them explain their answers.

## You Can Answer These Questions

You may want to have students do this activity as classwork or as homework.

1. a
2. c
3. c
4. c
5. b
6. b
7. b
8. b
9. a
10. a

## Exercises to Help You

### Using Modals: *can/could*

Draw a T-Chart on the board. On one side write statements using *can*. On the other side, write similar sentences using *could*.

> I *can* walk 20 miles in a day.
> Pakhom *could* walk 30 miles in a day.
>
> We *can* buy some land.
> The Chief *could* sell some land.

Explain that *can* is used to talk about what is possible now. Label the first column *Now*. Point out that *could* is used to talk about what was possible in the past; label the second column *Past*. You may want to have students look back through pages 147–149 for other examples of *can* and *could* to add to the chart.

Assign Exercises A, B, and C on pages 151–153. Students can work in pairs or groups to complete them as classwork or you can assign the exercises for homework.

*Exercise A*
Students' sentences will vary.

1. He was wearing a large fur hat and a large fur coat.
2. Pakhom gave the Chief a beautiful coat and five pounds of tea.
3. The price of the land was 500 rubles a day.
4. The Chief gave Pakhom a shovel.
5. He couldn't sleep because he kept thinking about the land.
6. Pakhom finally fell asleep just before dawn.
7. The Chief put his hat on the ground.
8. The helper gave Pakhom some bread and some water.

## Exercise B

1.  e    Pakhom gave some presents to the Chief.
2.  a    The Chief said Pakhom could choose a piece of land.
3.  d    Pakhom could have all the land that he walked around in a day.
4.  b    Pakhom thought he would get a huge piece of land.
5.  c    That night Pakhom had a strange dream.
6.  e    The next morning Pakhom woke up his helper.
7.  c    They walked until they came to the top of a hill.
8.  b    The Bashkirs had wonderful land.
9.  a    Pakhom could walk wherever he wanted to go.
10. d    He had to return before the sun set.

## Exercise C

1.  fur
2.  at once
3.  agree
4.  pocket
5.  shovel
6.  rent

### Using Possessive Pronouns

Write these pronouns on the board:

my    yours    his    its    our    their

Then write these sentences on the board.

The Chief had some land, but he sold _____ land.
I am from Mexico. _____ name is Luis.
The house is old. _____ windows are broken.
Jiwon and Ilmin have a car. _____ car is blue.
We study in this room. This is _____ classroom.
You have a book. This book is _____.

Check understanding by asking students to fill in the possessives in the correct sentences. As you go over the answers, point out the subject pronoun that corresponds to each possessive pronoun. Students can look for additional examples of the possessives in the story on pages 147–149.

Assign Exercises D, E, and F on pages 153–155.

## Exercise D

1.  his
2.  yours
3.  my
4.  our
5.  its
6.  their

## Exercise E

1.  The price was 500 rubles a day.
2.  That night Pakhom could not sleep.
3.  Pakhom had a strange dream.
4.  The Chief took off his fur hat.
5.  He put the hat on the ground.

## Exercise F

Students' sentences will vary.

## Sharing with Others

As a group, read the questions on page 155. Guide discussion of the questions. Help students explain their interpretation of the Chief's laugh. Make a list of students' predictions about the amount of land that Pakhom will get. Encourage students to give their own personal reaction by suggesting what they would do in Pakhom's place.

Give students a graphic organizer such as the Main Idea chart on page T1 to record their ideas before writing.

Have students share their writing by displaying it on a table or bulletin board or by reading it aloud. ■

# Land

## Warm Up

Use any or all of the activities below.

### Vocabulary: Understanding Meaning Associations

Write the word *greedy* on the board and explain or act out the meaning. As a group, write a definition for the word. Give students paper and have them draw a person or situation to illustrate the meaning of the word. You may want to have students consider if Pakhom is greedy.

## Read the Selection

Ask students to follow along on pages 156–157 of their books as you play CD track 48 or read aloud lines 1–35. Check students' understanding of the passage.

1. How far did Pakhom walk before digging the first hole?
2. Why did he look back at the hill? How did the people look?
3. Why did Pakhom take off his coat and boots? Do you think this was a good idea? Why or why not?
4. How did Pakhom feel at noon? What did he do? Then how did he feel?

Check that students understand key vocabulary in the selection. Ask students if they need to revise any of their predictions.

Play CD track 49 or read lines 36–62 on page 157. Check comprehension of the passage by using any or all of the following questions.

1. What did the land that was in front of Pakhom look like?
2. Did Pakhom walk a long distance? Why do you think so?
3. When the sun was beginning to set, where was Pakhom?
4. Why was Pakhom worried?
5. When did Pakhom begin to run? Why was he running?

Complete the reading for lines 63–103 on pages 157–158 or play CD track 50. Use any or all of these questions to check students' understanding.

1. How do you know that Pakhom was greedy?
2. When Pakhom saw the Chief, what did he remember?
3. Where was Pakhom when it got dark? How did he feel?
4. Did Pakhom get to the top on time? Did Pakhom get a lot of land or a little?
5. Why didn't Pakhom move? How much land did Pakhom need at the end?

Stop and allow students to think about the conclusion. Encourage them to check if their predictions about the story were correct.

### Model a Strategy: Understanding Irony

Say: "At the beginning of the story Pakhom only had an acre of land. Then he bought a lot of land from the Bashkirs. But at the end of the story he needed only six feet of land. He thought he needed more, but when he got it he didn't need it anymore. It was because he got so much land that he died, and it was because he died that he didn't need the land. We call that kind of situation ironic. *Ironic* means that what happens is very different from what we would expect to happen.

# You Can Answer These Questions

This activity can be assigned as class-work or as homework.

1. b        6. a
2. a        7. a
3. b        8. b
4. c        9. c
5. c        10. a

# Exercises to Help You

## Identifying Verb Tenses: Past, Present, Future

Write on the board:

He *walked* 3 miles.
He *walks* 3 miles.
He *will walk* 3 miles.

Ask students to point out which sentences can be used to talk about the past, present, and future. Write the tense words after the appropriate sentences. Help students explain how they determined the tenses based on the verb forms. Read or say other sentences and have students identify the verb tenses. Alternatively, ask students to look through the selection on pages 156–158 for examples of each of the verb tenses.

Students can do Exercises A, B, C, and D on pages 160–163. You may want to arrange students in pairs or groups to complete the exercises as classwork or assign them for homework.

*Exercise A*
Students' sentences will vary.

1. Pakhom walked toward the east.
2. Pakhom took off his boots to make it easier to walk.
3. The sun was beginning to set.
4. His feet were cut and his legs felt weak.
5. He threw away the water and the bread.
6. They were shouting at him to keep running.
7. Pakhom remembered his dream.
8. Pakhom was dead.
9. The helper dug a grave.
10. It was six feet long.

*Exercise B*

1. b  Pakhom carried the shovel over his shoulder.
2. d  He walked for a mile and then dug the first hole.
3. e  Pakhom turned and looked back toward the hill.
4. c  The people on the hill looked very small.
5. a  Pakhom saw that the sun was beginning to set.
6. b  Pakhom began to run back to the hill.
7. e  His heart was beating very loudly.
8. a  He heard the Bashkirs yelling at him to hurry.
9. c  Finally his fingers touched the hat.
10. d  Pakhom did not move because he was dead.

*Exercise C*

1. rise        5. direction
2. marched     6. waving
3. pile        7. possible
4. boots       8. flowing

### Exercise D

| | | | |
|---|---|---|---|
| 1. | Past | 9. | Present |
| 2. | Past | 10. | Past |
| 3. | Future | 11. | Future |
| 4. | Past | 12. | Present |
| 5. | Present | 13. | Present |
| 6. | Present | 14. | Past |
| 7. | Future | 15. | Past |
| 8. | Future | | |

## Changing Statements to Questions

List these question words on the board:

who     what     where     why

how     how far     how much

Then write several sentences and invite students to change the sentences to questions using any of the question words.

> Pakhom ran 3 miles.
> *How far* did Pakhom run?
> *Who* ran 3 miles?

> The Chief laughed.
> *What* did the Chief do?
> *Who* laughed?

Help students explain how they formed the questions. Point out word order and verb forms in the questions, the use of *did*, and information that is left out (the answer to the question).

Assign Exercises E and F on pages 164–166.

### Exercise E

1. What did Pakhom see?
2. What made him feel better?
3. How was his heart beating?
4. How far did Pakhom walk?
5. What did Pakhom eat?
6. Where was Pakhom?
7. Who saw the Chief?
8. What did Pakhom remember?
9. Why could they see the sun?
10. How much land did the helper need?

### Exercise F

Students' sentences will vary.

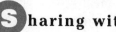 ## haring with Others

Read the questions on page 166 together and help students draw conclusions about what killed Pakhom and about the story's ending.

Have students choose one question to write about. Give them a copy of the Main Idea chart on page T1 for recording their ideas before writing.

Display students' work or have students share their writing aloud. ■

# Answers for Unit 5: Land

1. Pakhom and his helper traveled for seven days.
2. Pakhom fell down and died.
3. A traveler told Pakhom about the land of the Bashkirs.
4. Pakhom walked all day to buy a lot of land.
5. A traveler told Pakhom about the land of the Bashkirs.
6. Pakhom and his helper traveled for seven days.
7. Pakhom walked all day to buy a lot of land.
8. Pakhom fell down and died.

| | | | |
|---|---|---|---|
| 9. | own | 14. | My |
| 10. | greedy | 15. | their |
| 11. | whispered | 16. | our |
| 12. | gifts | 17. | them |
| 13. | price | | |

18. talked
19. drank
20. sold
21. Who talked together for a long time?
22. What did the traveler drink before he left?
23. How much (money) did the Bashkirs sell their land for?

**Name** _____  **Date** _____

# Land

**A s s e s s m e n t**

**A.** **Finish the sentences by drawing lines from the first part to the second part. Write the complete sentences on the lines below, in the same order they happened in the story.**

1. Pakhom and his helper                    and died.
2. Pakhom fell down                          the land of the Bashkirs.
3. A traveler told Pakhom about              to buy a lot of land.
4. Pakhom walked all day                     traveled for seven days.

5. _____

6. _____

7. _____

8. _____

**B.** **Complete each sentence by filling in the correct word.**

gifts        price        greedy        own        whispered

9. Pakhom did not _____ a large farm.

10. Don't take too much. Don't be _____!

11. The man _____ in the Chief's ear.

12. Pakhom bought some _____ in a town.

13. How much does it cost? The _____ is $5.00.

**C.** **Fill in each blank, using an object pronoun or a possessive.**

me   you   him   her   us   them   my   yours   his   her   it   our   their

14. Pakhom said, "_____ farm is too small."

15. The Bashkirs put _____ tents near the river.

16. The Chief said, "We will sell some of _____ land to you."

17. Did he give the money to the Bashkirs? Yes, he gave _____ the money.

**D.** **Fill in each blank, using the past tense of the verb in parentheses. Then change the sentences into questions. Write the questions on the lines below.**

18. Pakhom and the traveler _____ together for a long time. (talk)

19. The traveler _____ some tea before he left. (drink)

20. The Bashkirs _____ their land for very little money. (sell)

21. Who _____?

22. What _____?

23. How much _____?